# talking heads

Ian Gurvitz

ISBN-10: 1539098206
ISBN-13: 978-1539098201

## table of contents

## introduction | talking heads

This is not art in the sense that these drawings are the result of a unique creative vision. They are accidental flights of fantasy – spontaneous, right brain meanderings with a mind of their own.

I started drawing in TV writers' rooms. During rewrites I would doodle on my script pages, either to keep my mind alive or to keep my head from exploding. Anyone who's been in a room at midnight, staring at a sea of blank faces all searching for the same insight, knows this experience. Most of the drawings were tossed out at the end of the night, along with stacks of cold pizza but, occasionally, one would take on a distinct character, or style, or evoke a mood or emotion. Those were interesting enough to keep, and eventually enough of an incentive to buy sketch pads and pens, and pursue it outside of work.

I'm not an artist. Having read *Drawing on the Right Side of the Brain*, and taken some art classes, I knew the trick was to draw without trying to draw — to let go of any desire for a specific result and just let it happen. The "not-doing" of it became an interesting exercise. If I let go, it occasionally went somewhere interesting. If I got too deliberate, the results were forced. Sometimes, when I felt stuck in a familiar pattern, I'd try to break out of my head by taking a different color pen, and attacking the page randomly. Once in a while, I got in the zone. Though, as with all attempts at mindlessness, once you become aware of it, it's gone.

Of the 100 or so drawings I've done to date, these seemed to express a unique attitude or emotion. I then added captions in an attempt to capture or enhance the mood. Whether there's anything Freudian going on in the darker images, I have no idea.

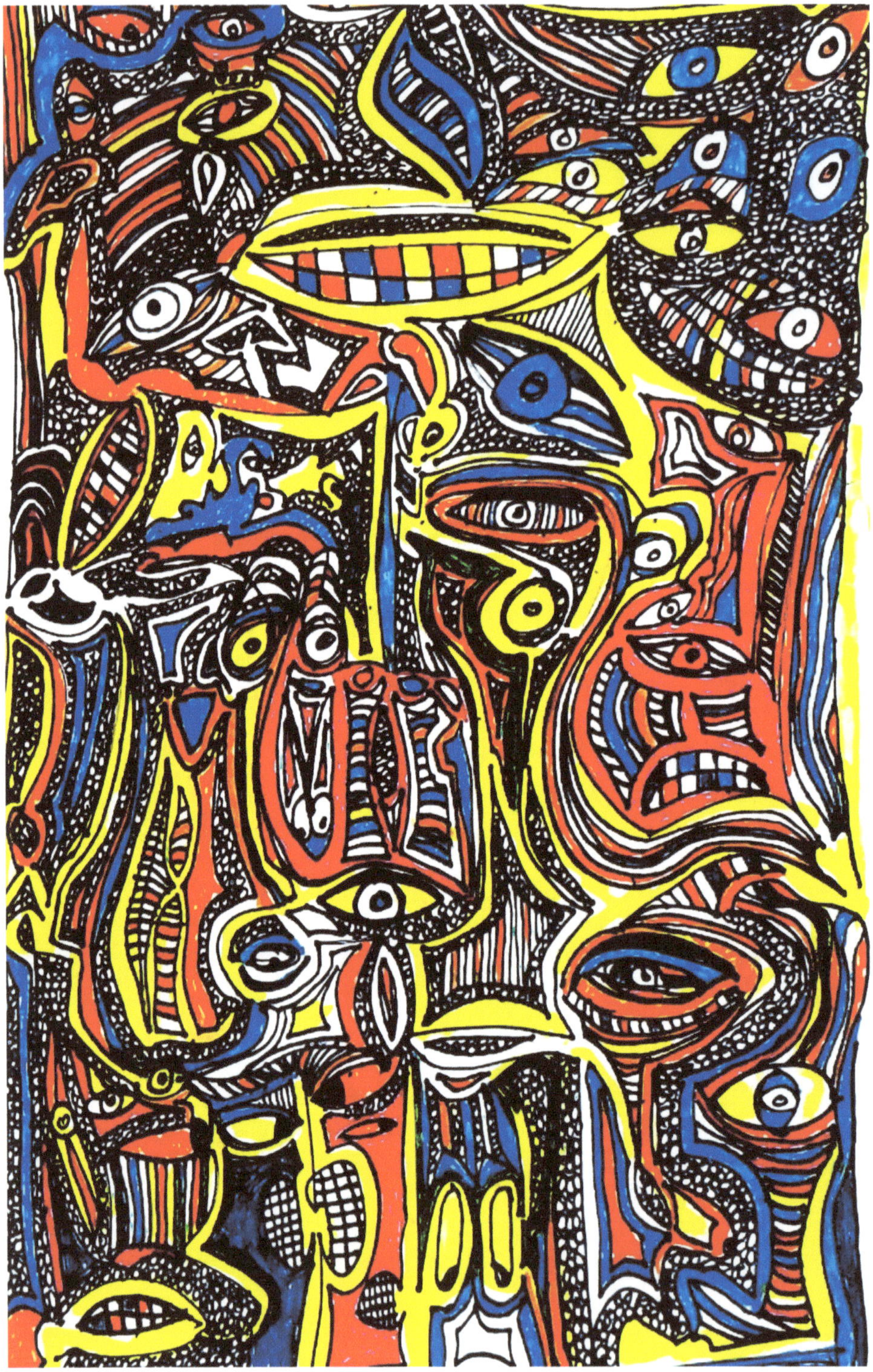

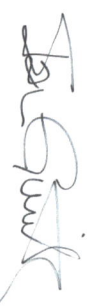

*Tempers were running hot at the Picasso family reunion.*

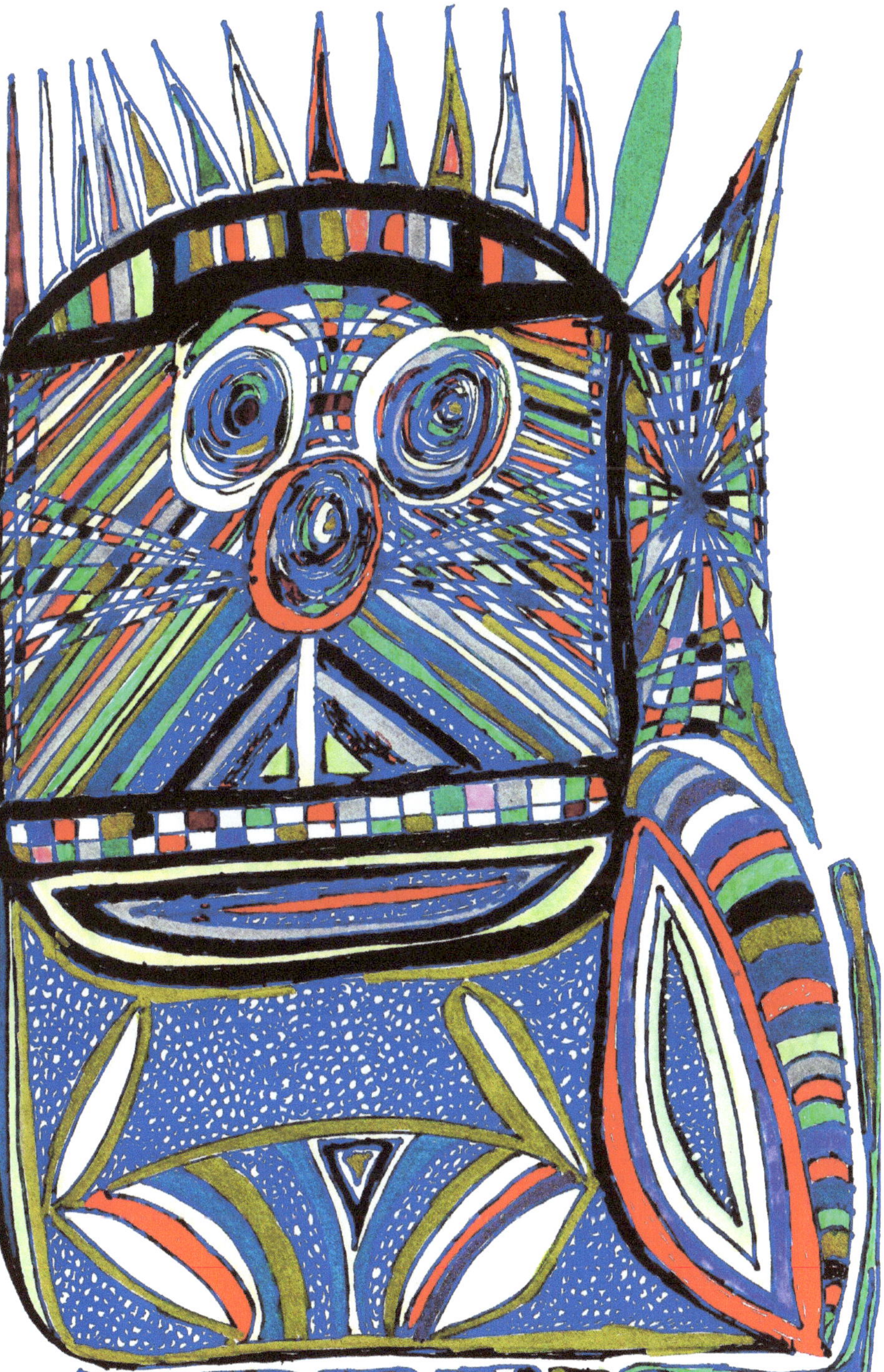

*I am not your cat!*
*I'm my own cat!*
*NOW, FILL MY FUCKING BOWL!*

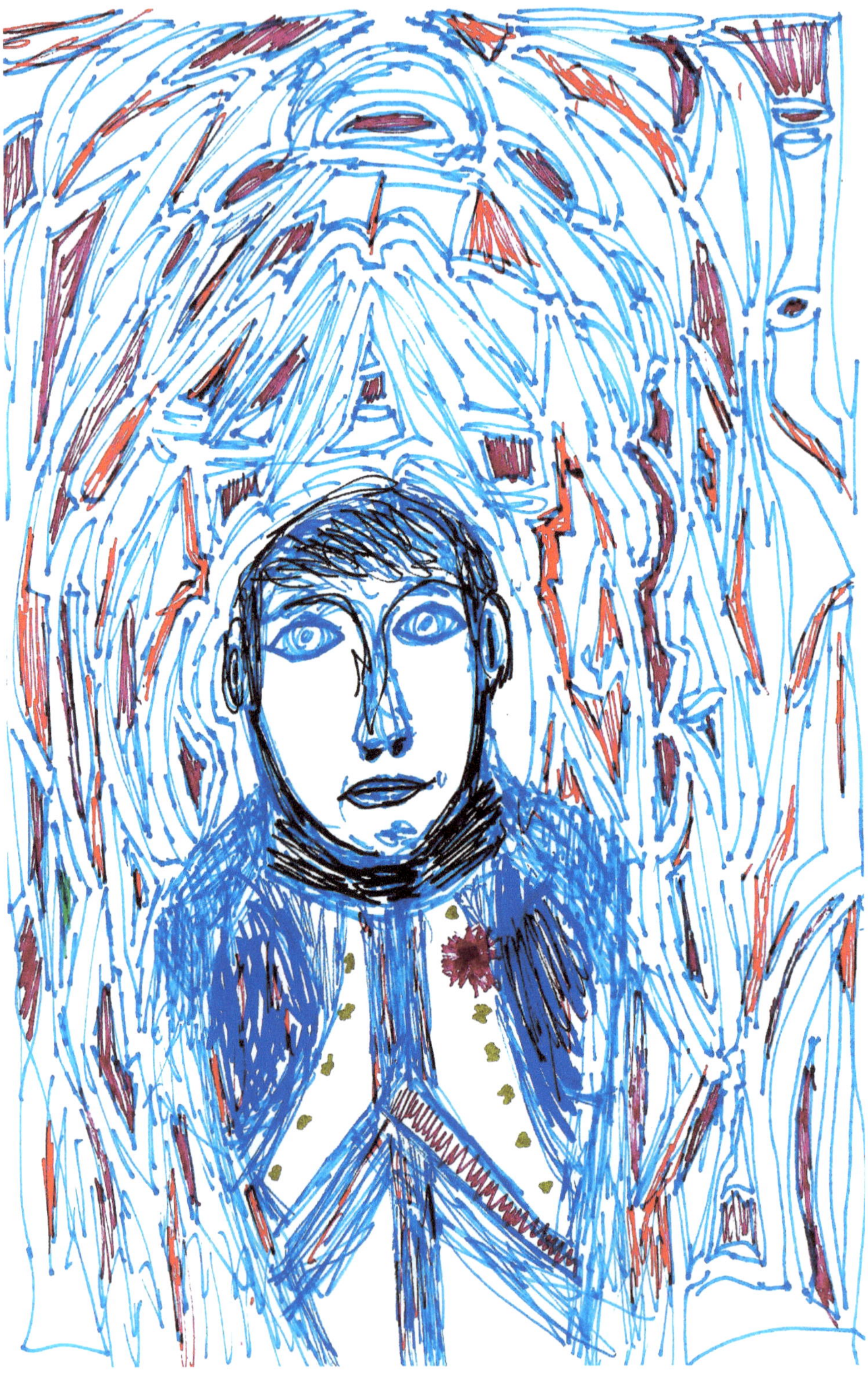

*Je ne suis pas un complexe!*
*Je ne suis pas un dessert!*
*Je suis un général!*

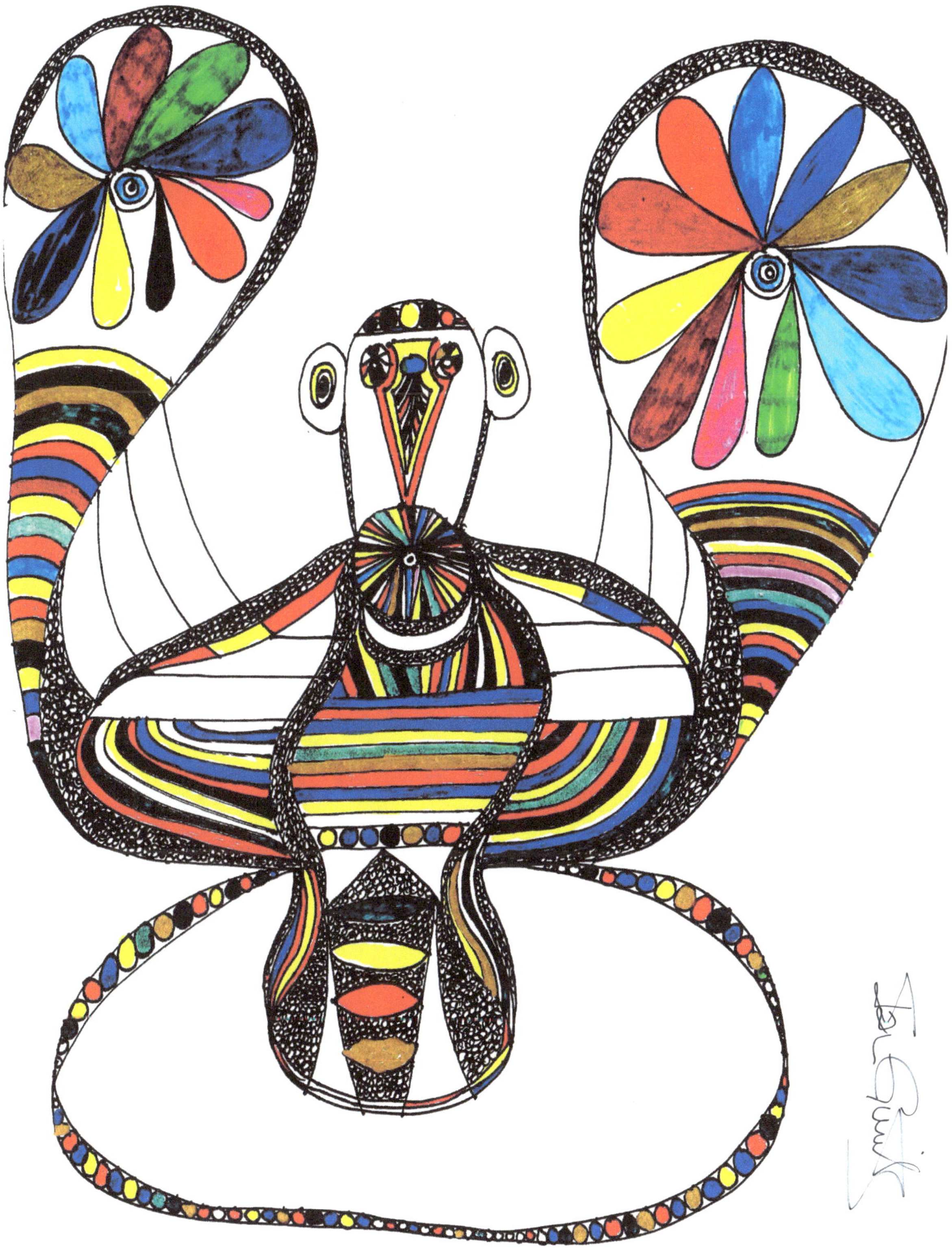

Don't shoot! I have balloon arms!

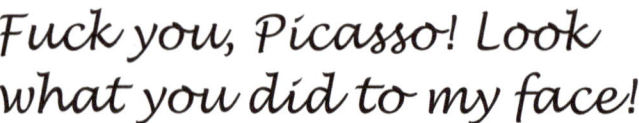

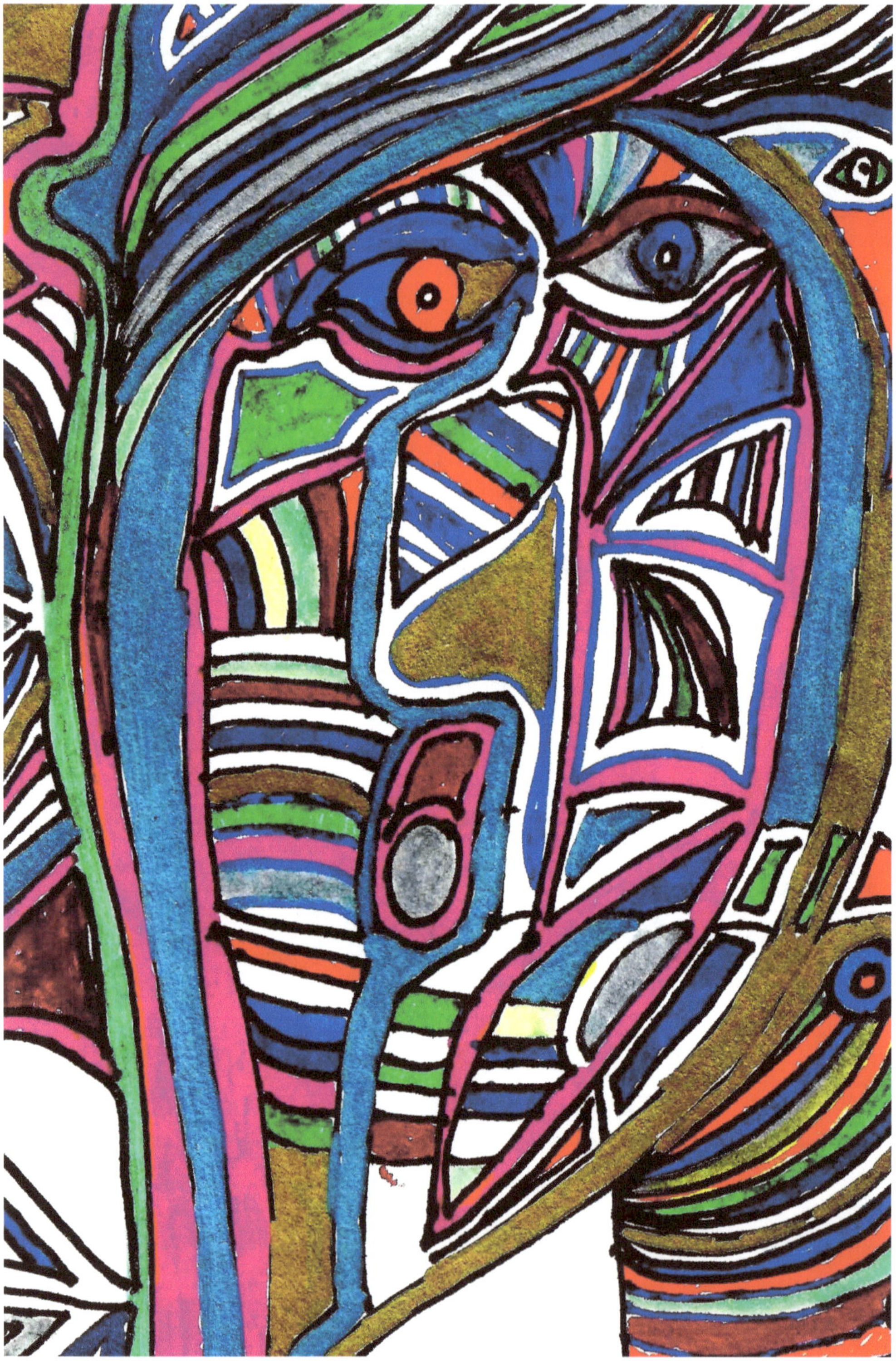

*Fuck you, Picasso! Look what you did to my face!*

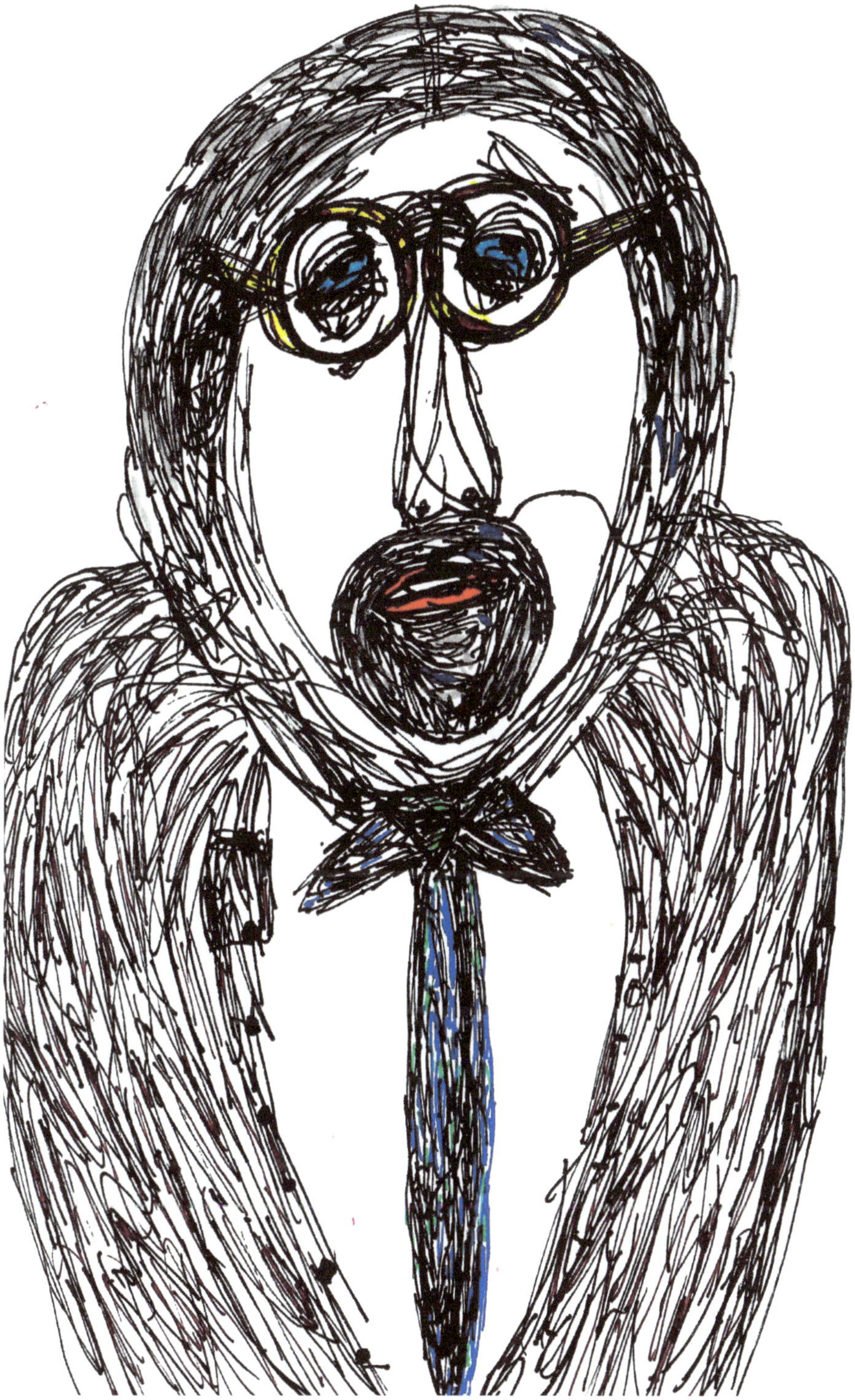

After a distinguished career as a psychotherapist, Dr. Gelman decided to write a book, laying out his observations on human behavior, but the only theory he could come up with was that people were just fucking crazy.

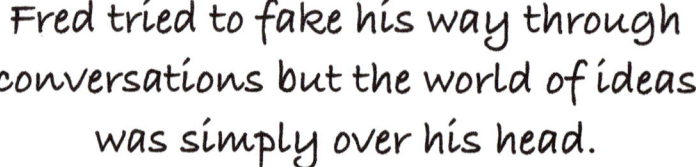

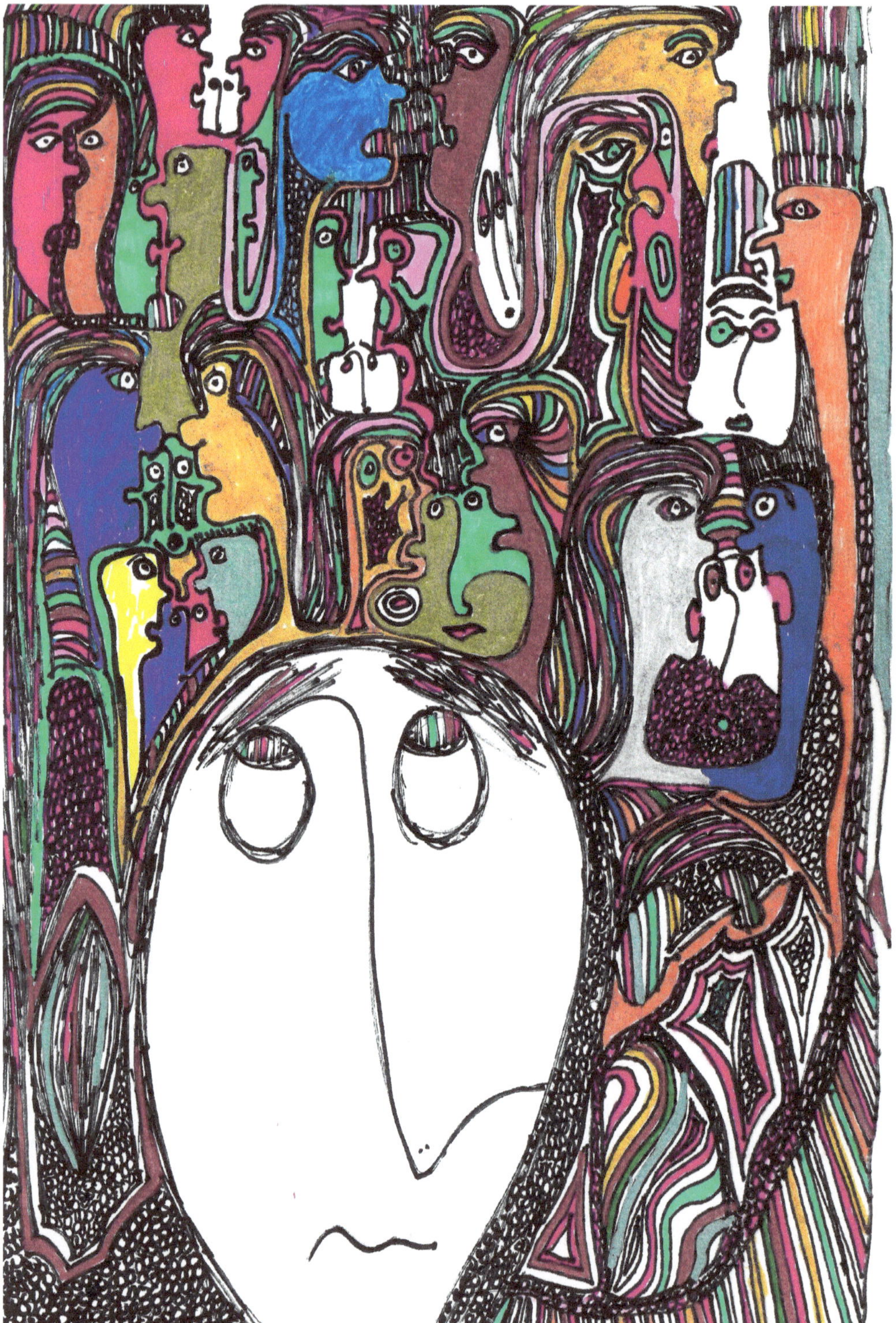

Fred tried to fake his way through conversations but the world of ideas was simply over his head.

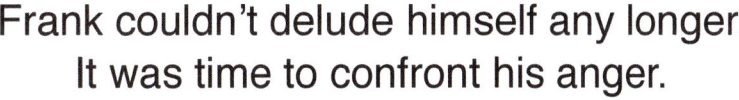

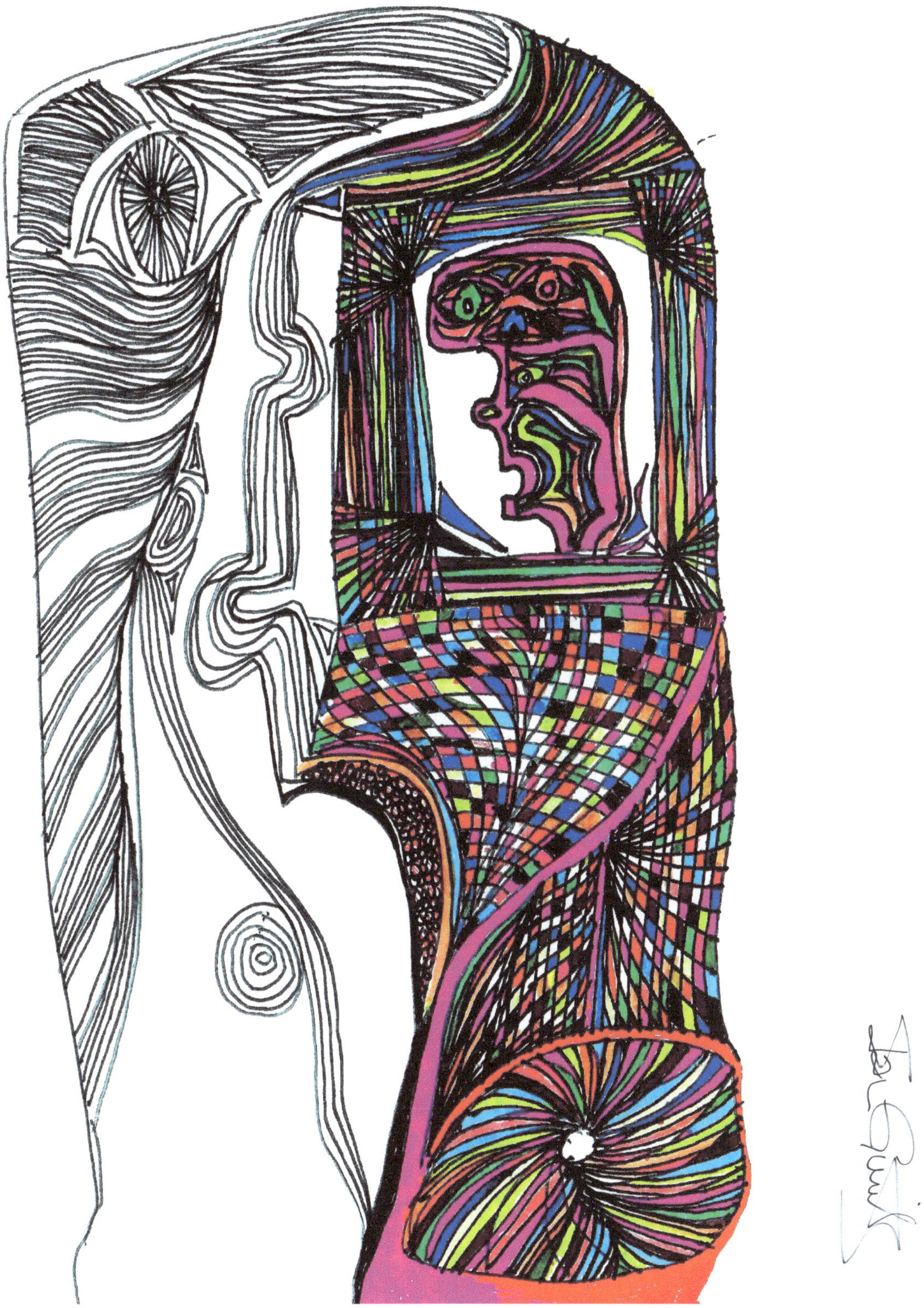

Frank couldn't delude himself any longer.
It was time to confront his anger.

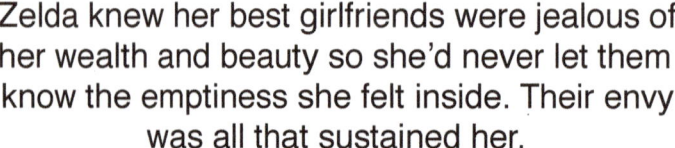

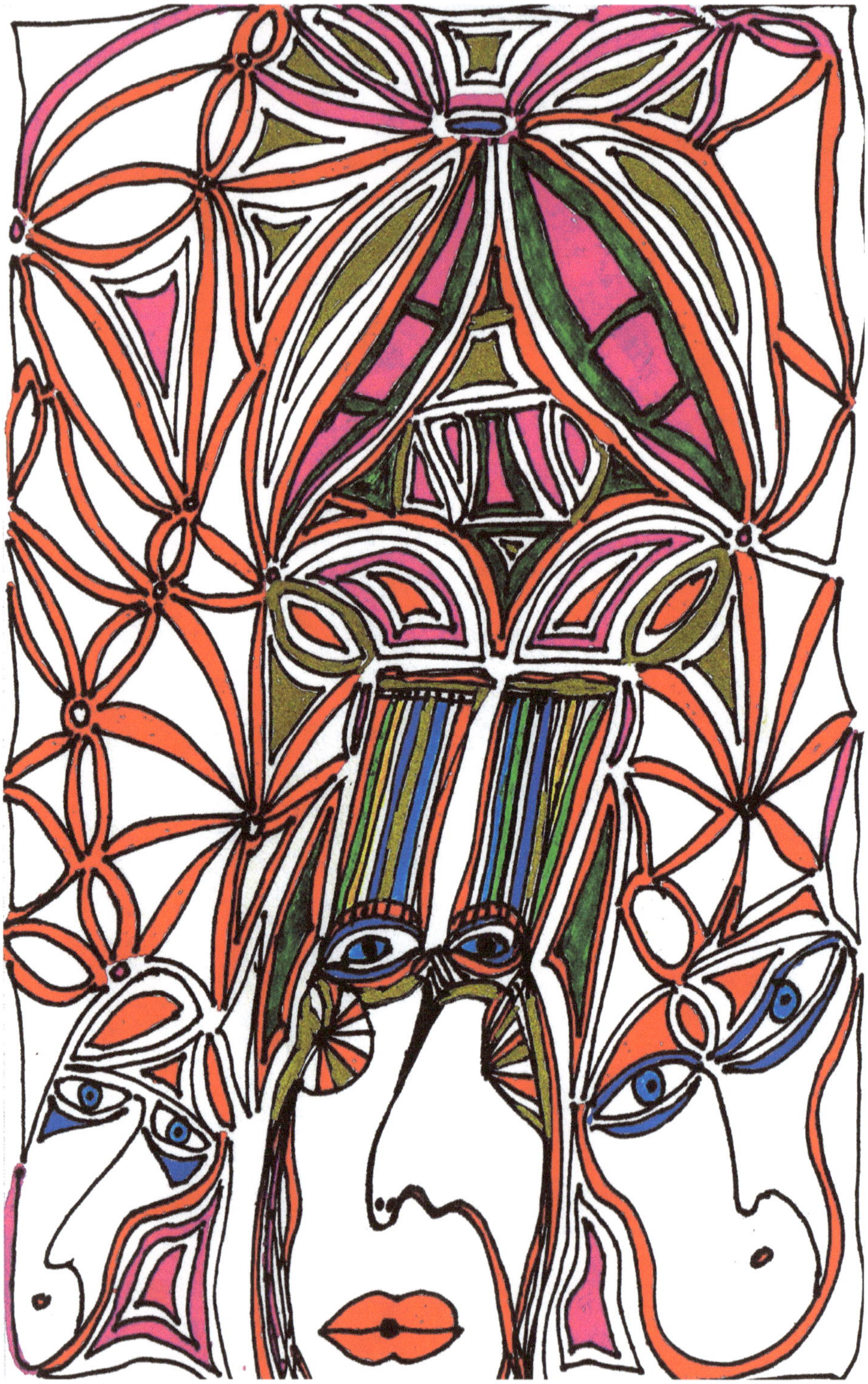

Zelda knew her best girlfriends were jealous of her wealth and beauty so she'd never let them know the emptiness she felt inside. Their envy was all that sustained her.

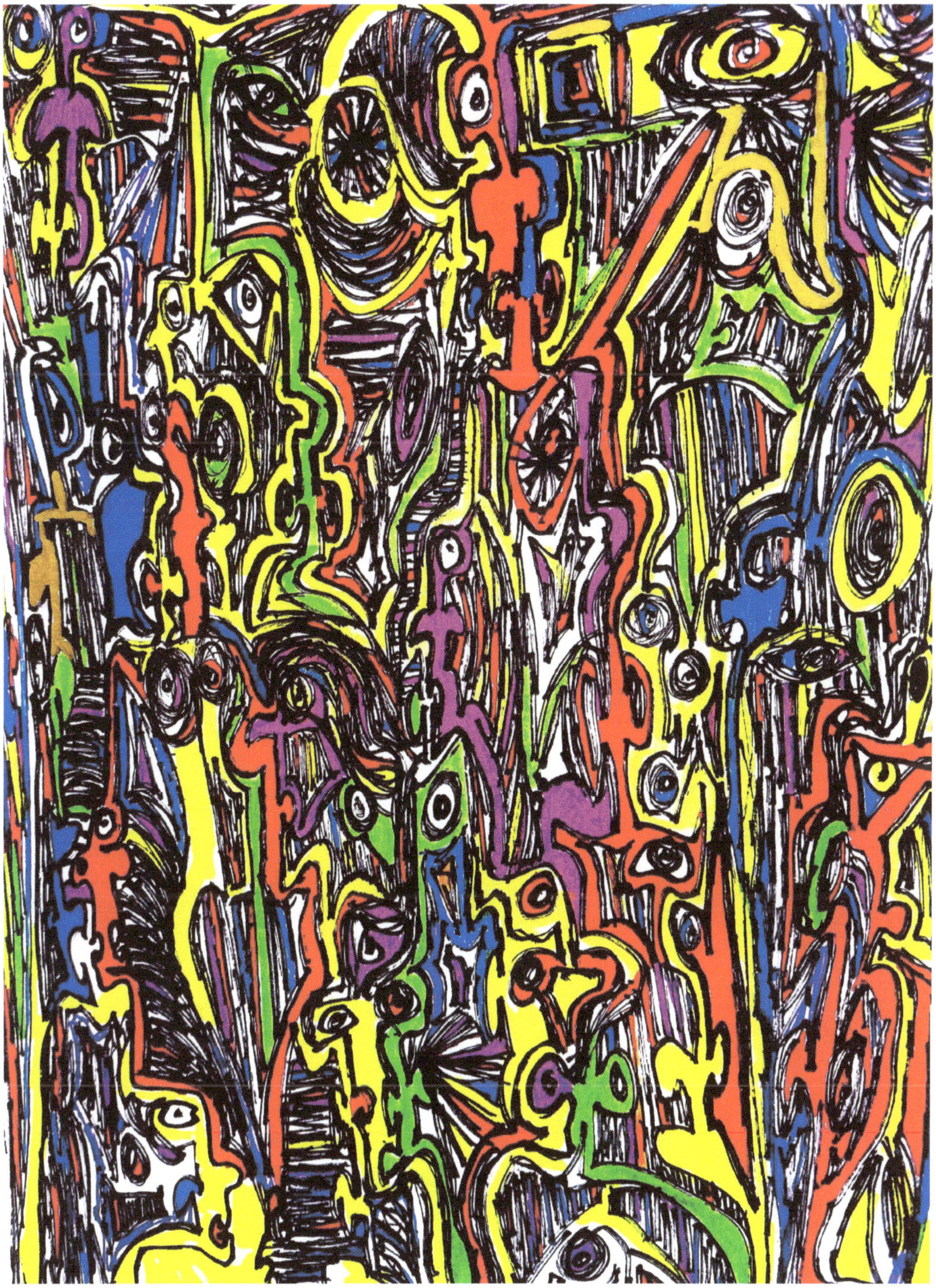

*Everybody's got an opinion.*

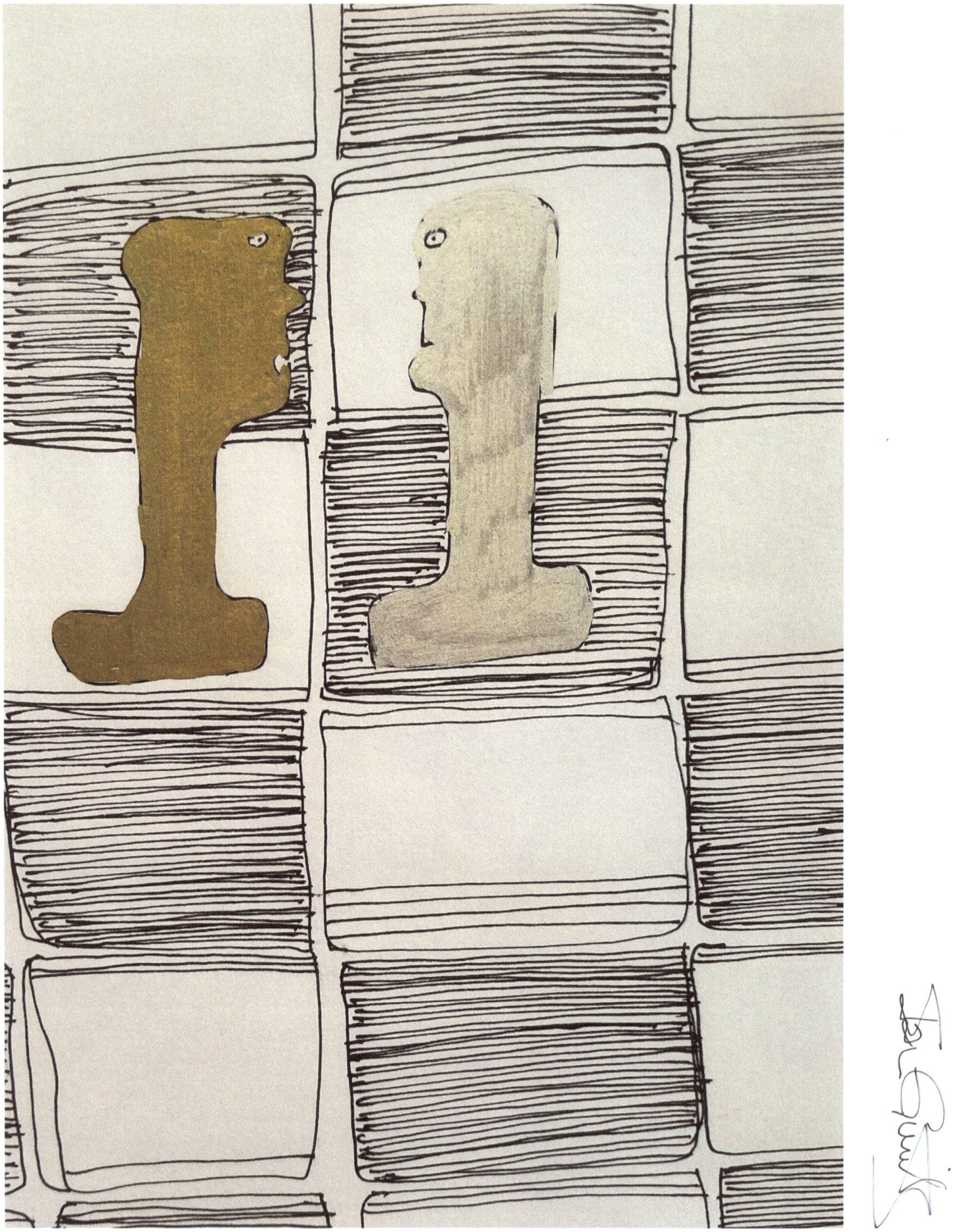

"You can delude yourself into thinking you've got free will but you're really just a pawn in someone else's game."

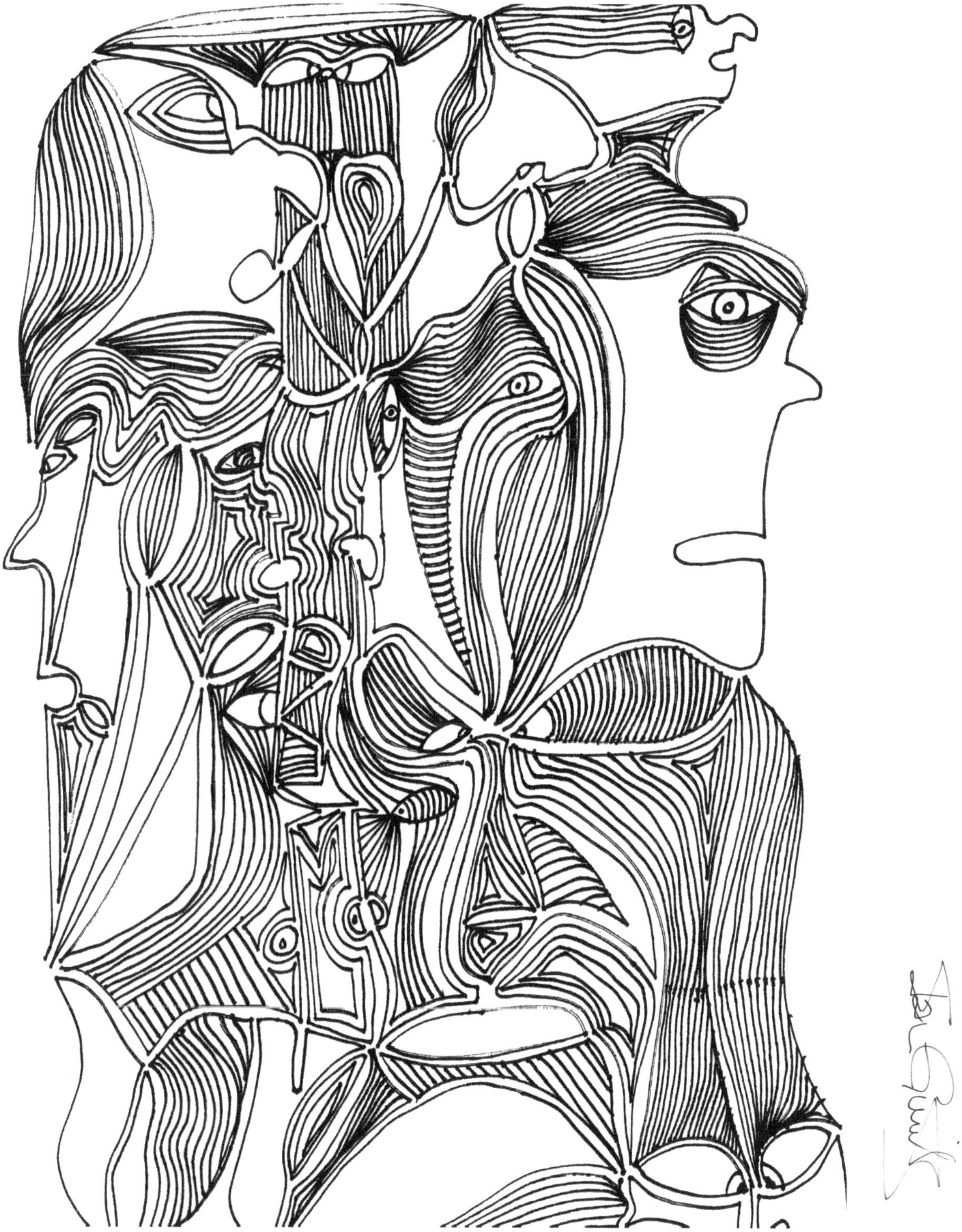

talking heads

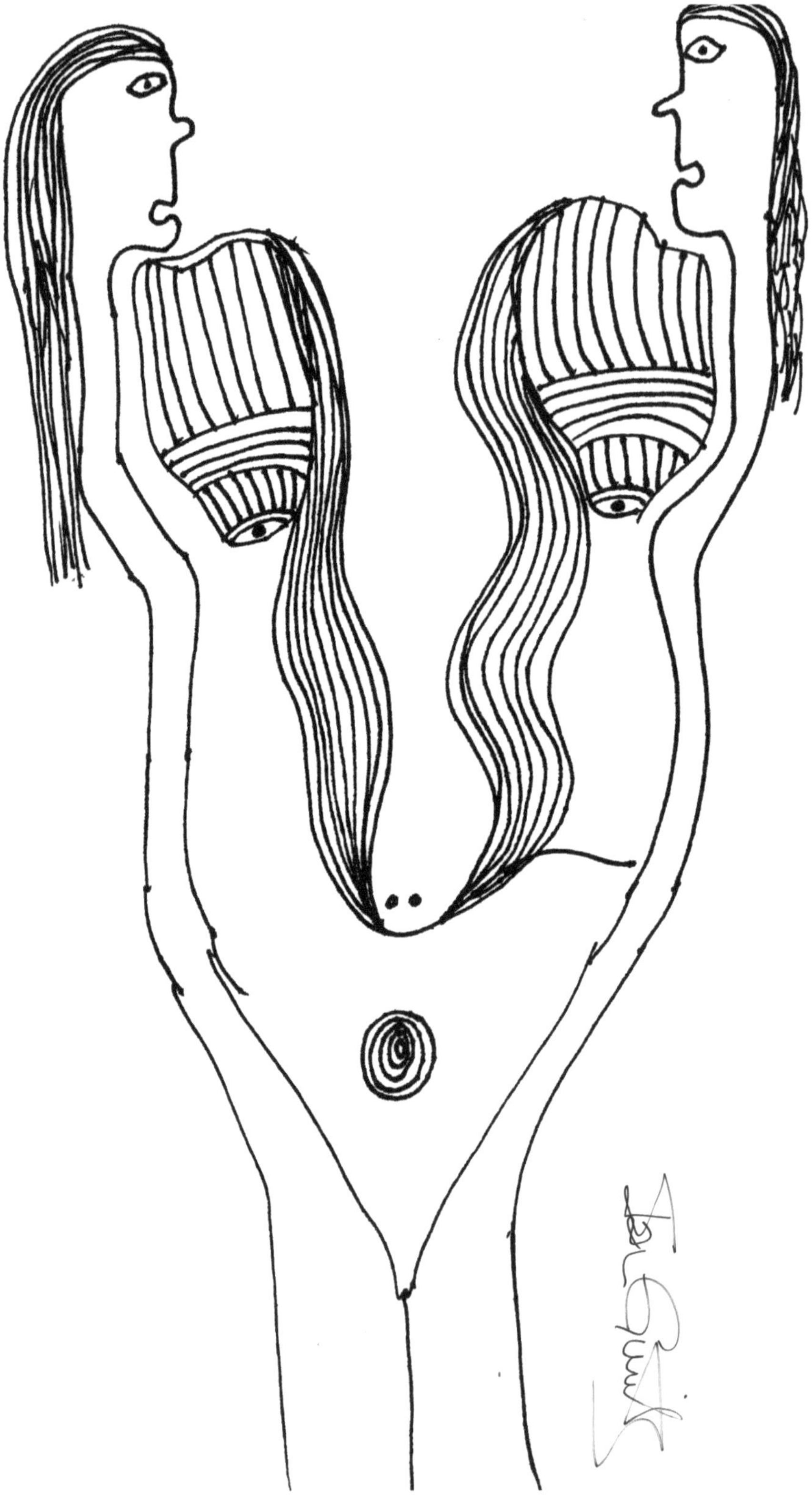

women troubles

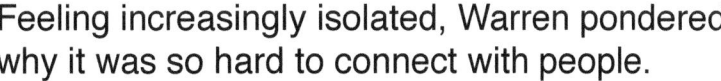

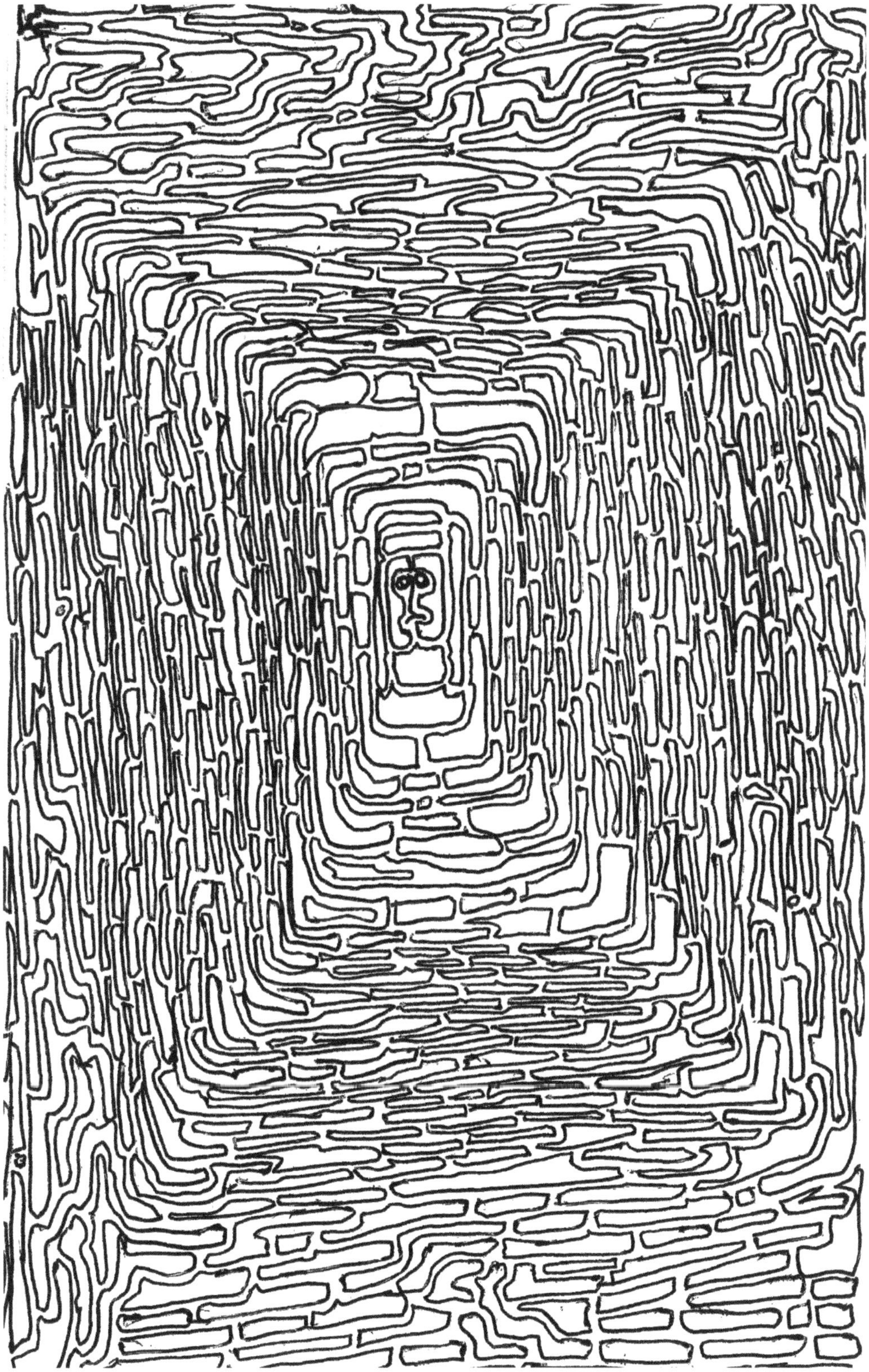

Feeling increasingly isolated, Warren pondered why it was so hard to connect with people.

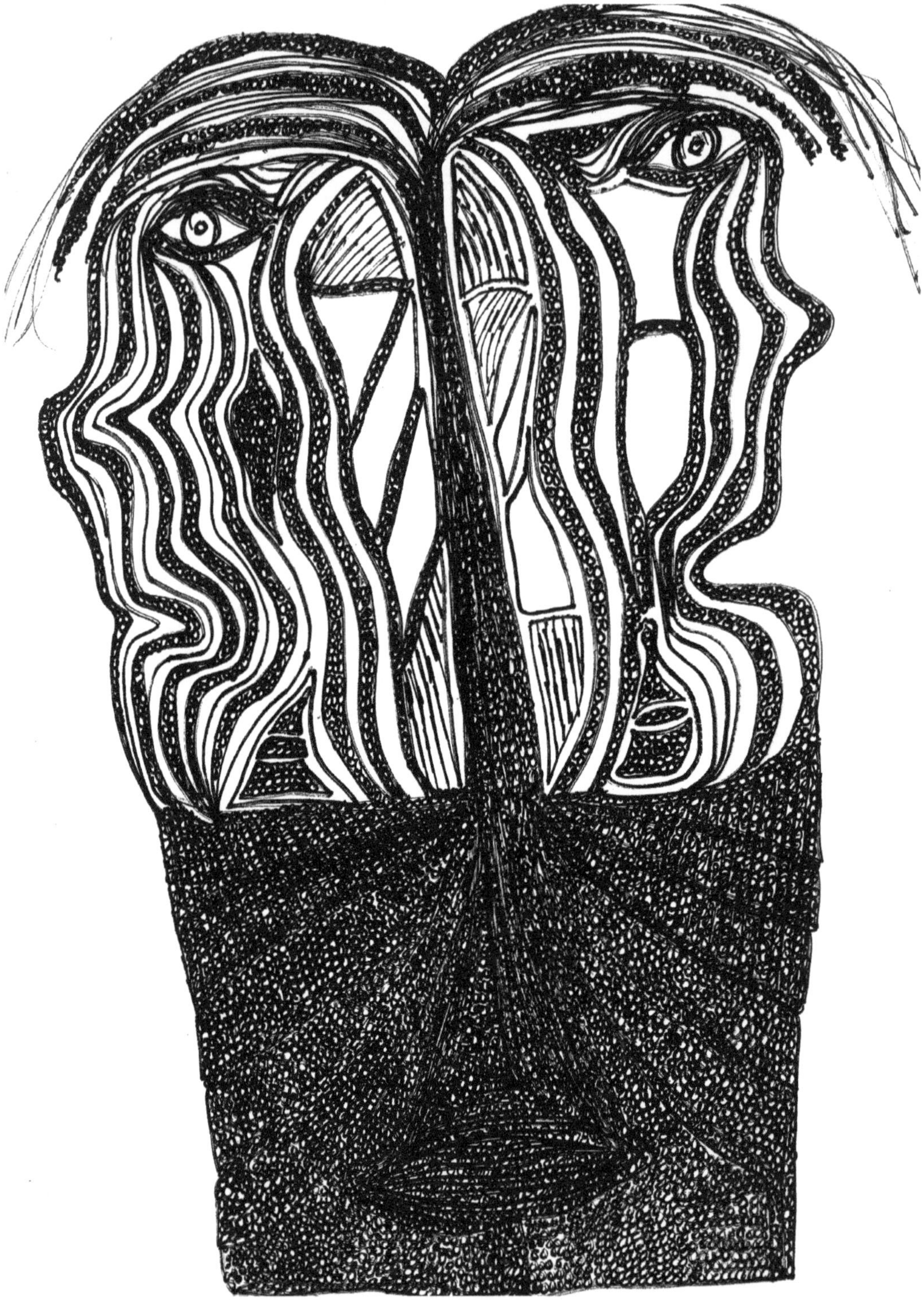

Though joined at the head, Bert and Barry
hadn't spoken in 40 years.

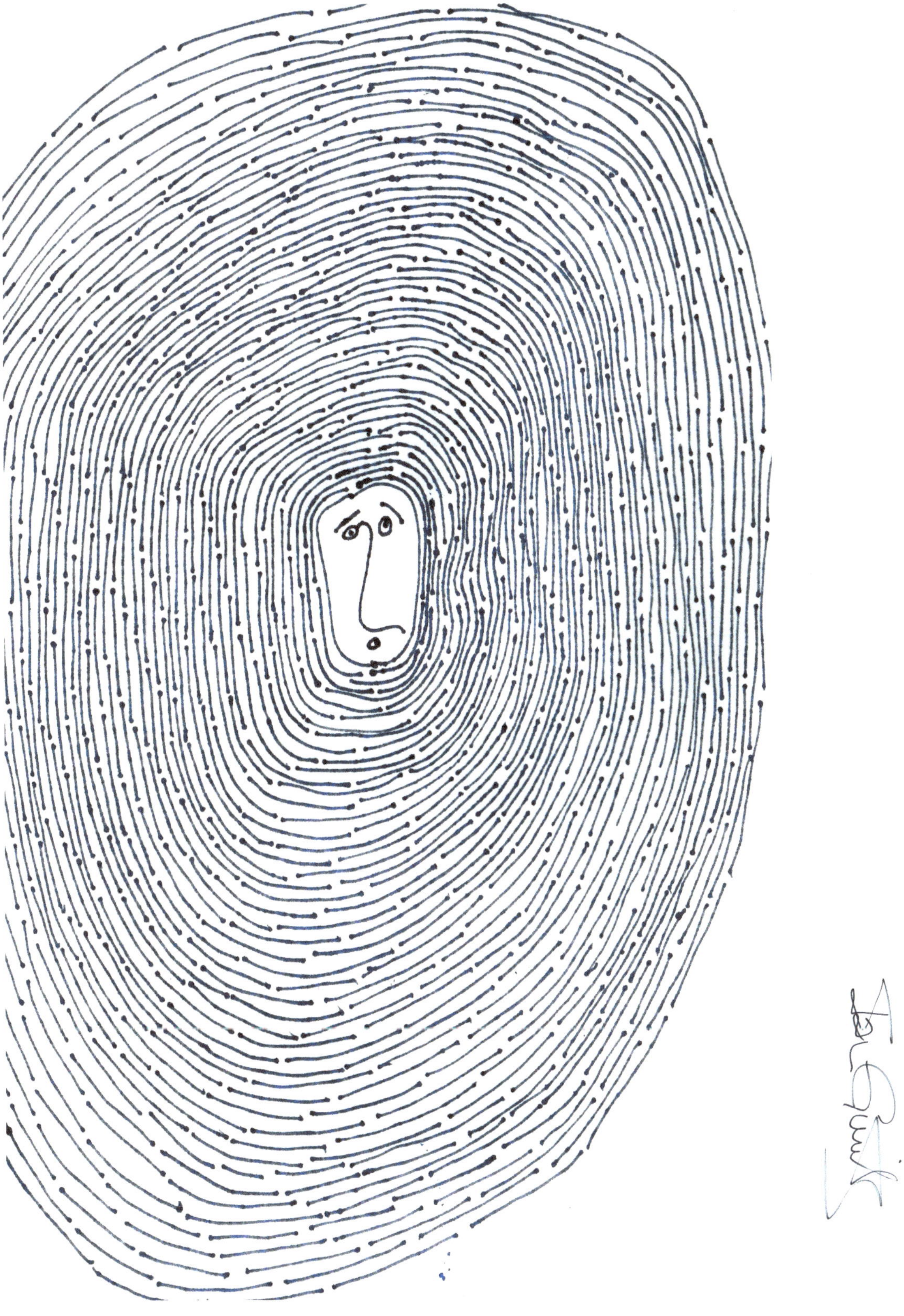

Evan was so nondescript, even his fingerprint wasn't unique.

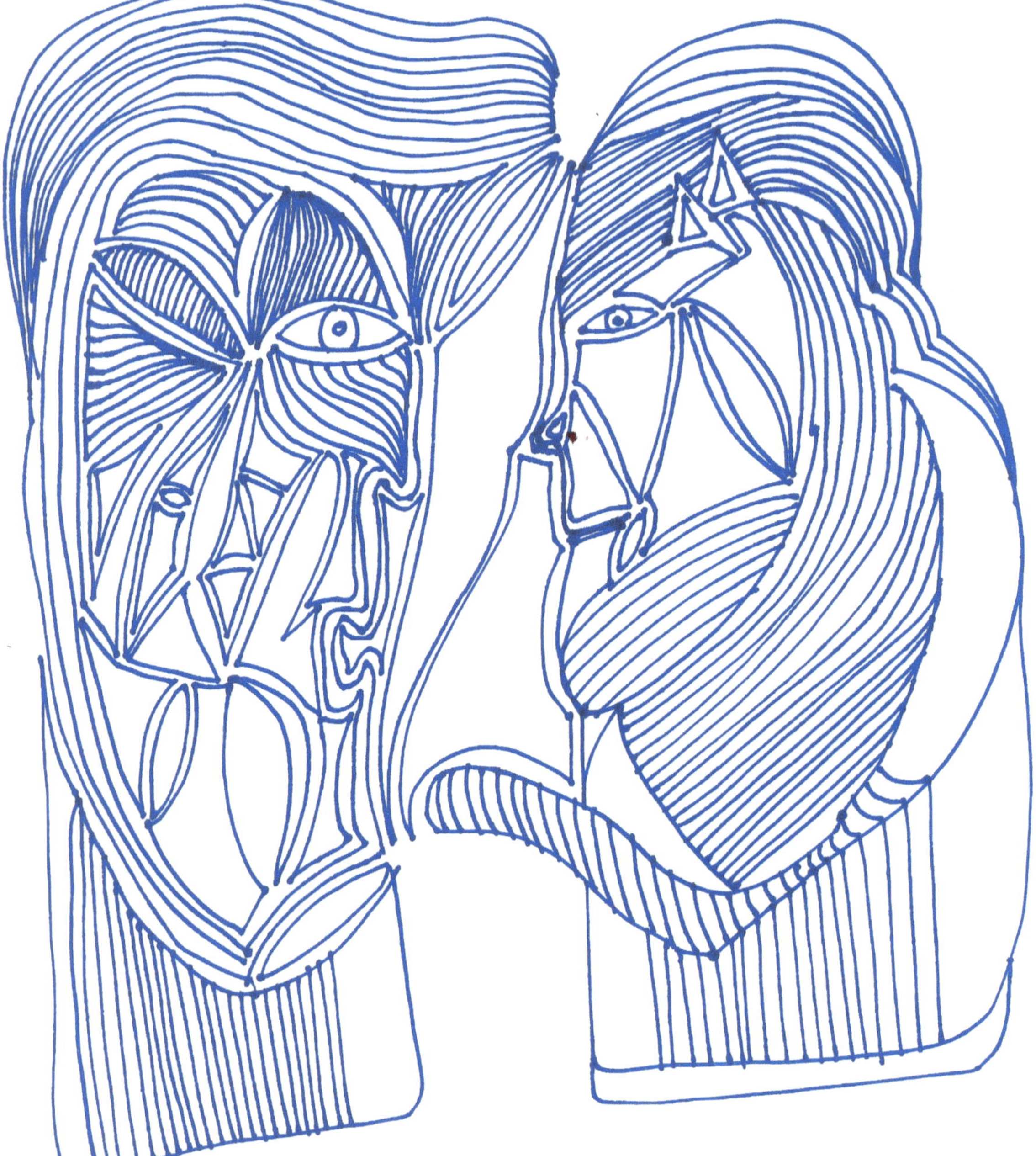

*After years of petty spats and domestic squabbles, Barry and his cat, Tibbles went to therapy, where they learned to accept their differences and respect each other's boundaries.*

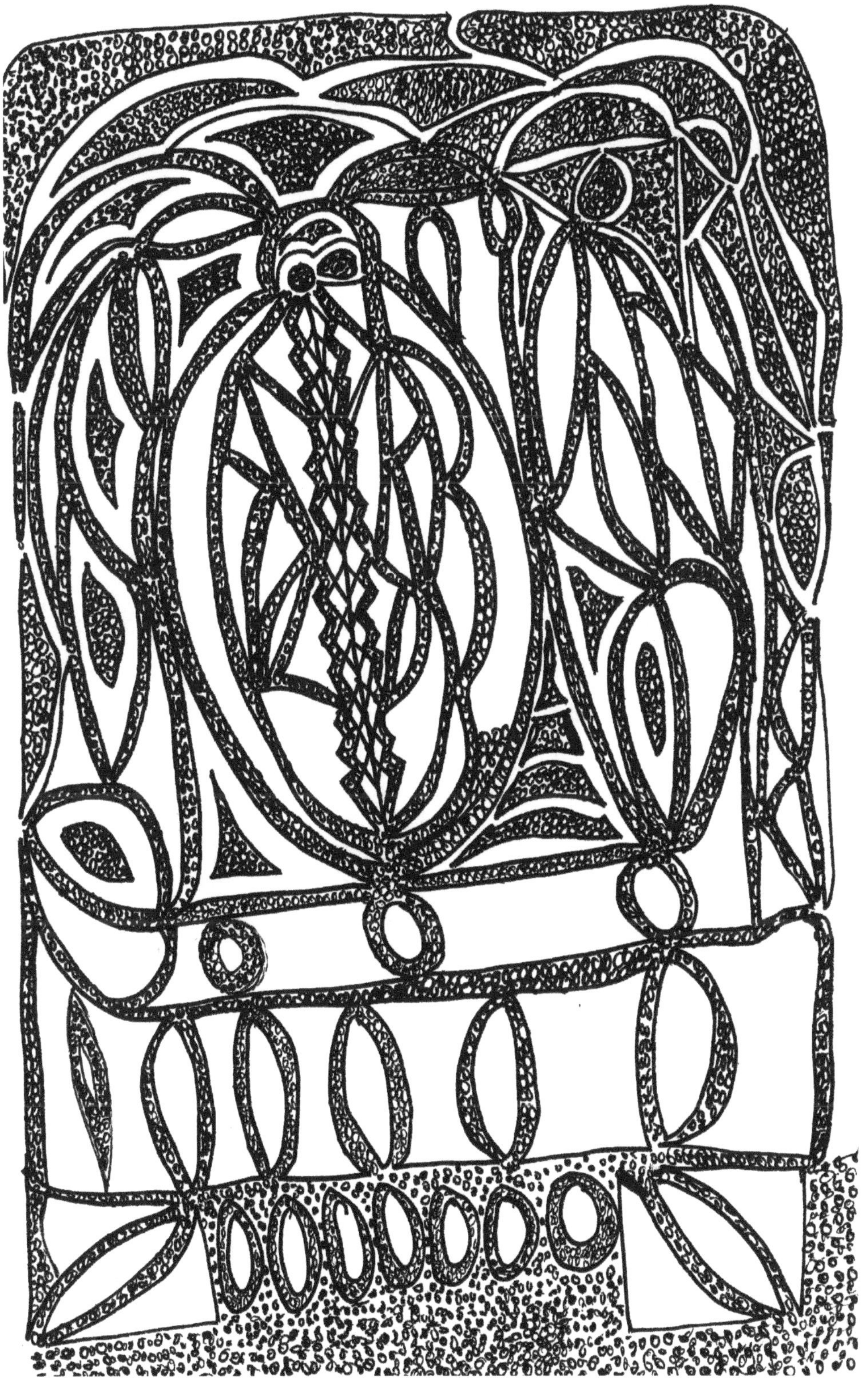

*elephant in chains*

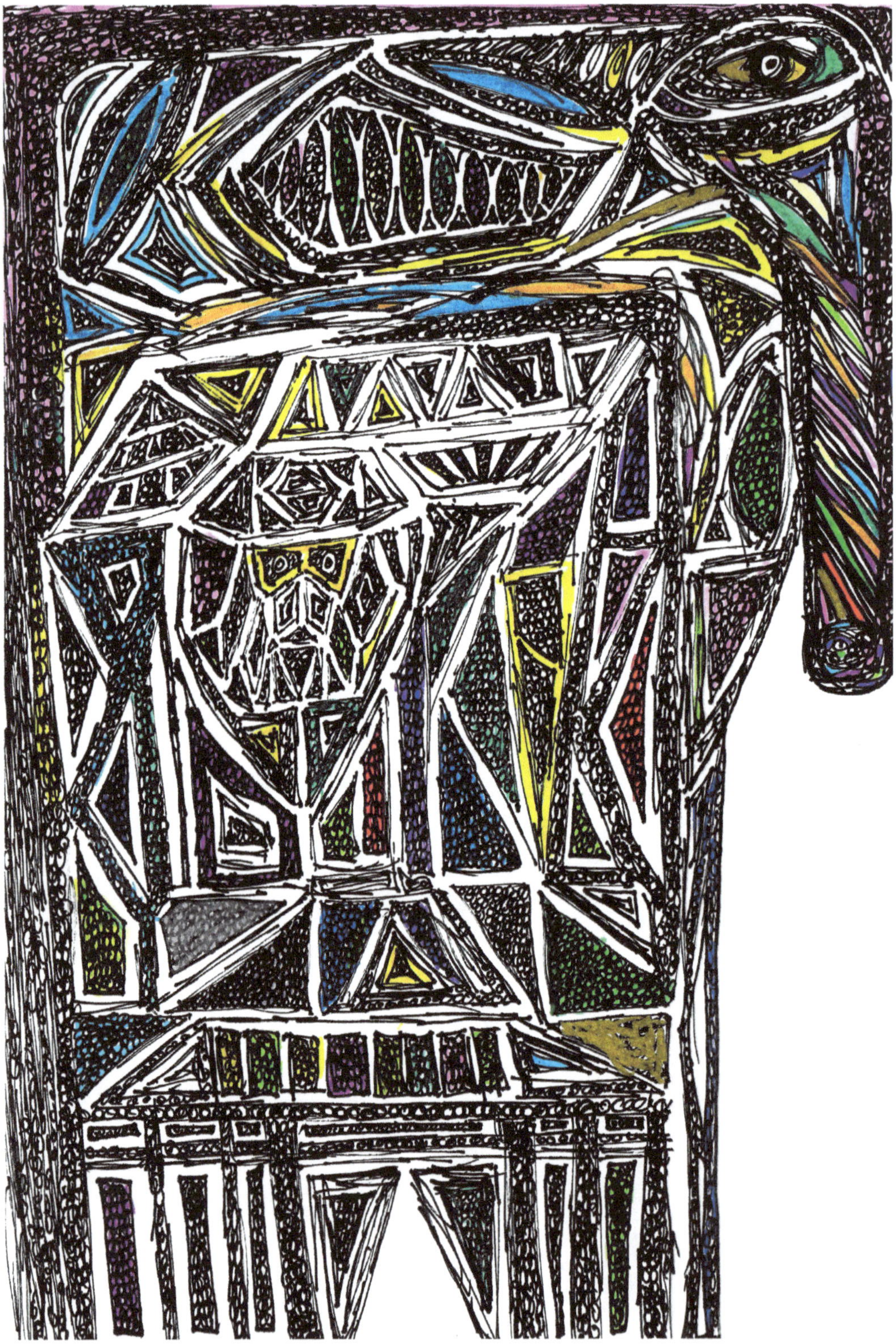

colorful elephant in chains

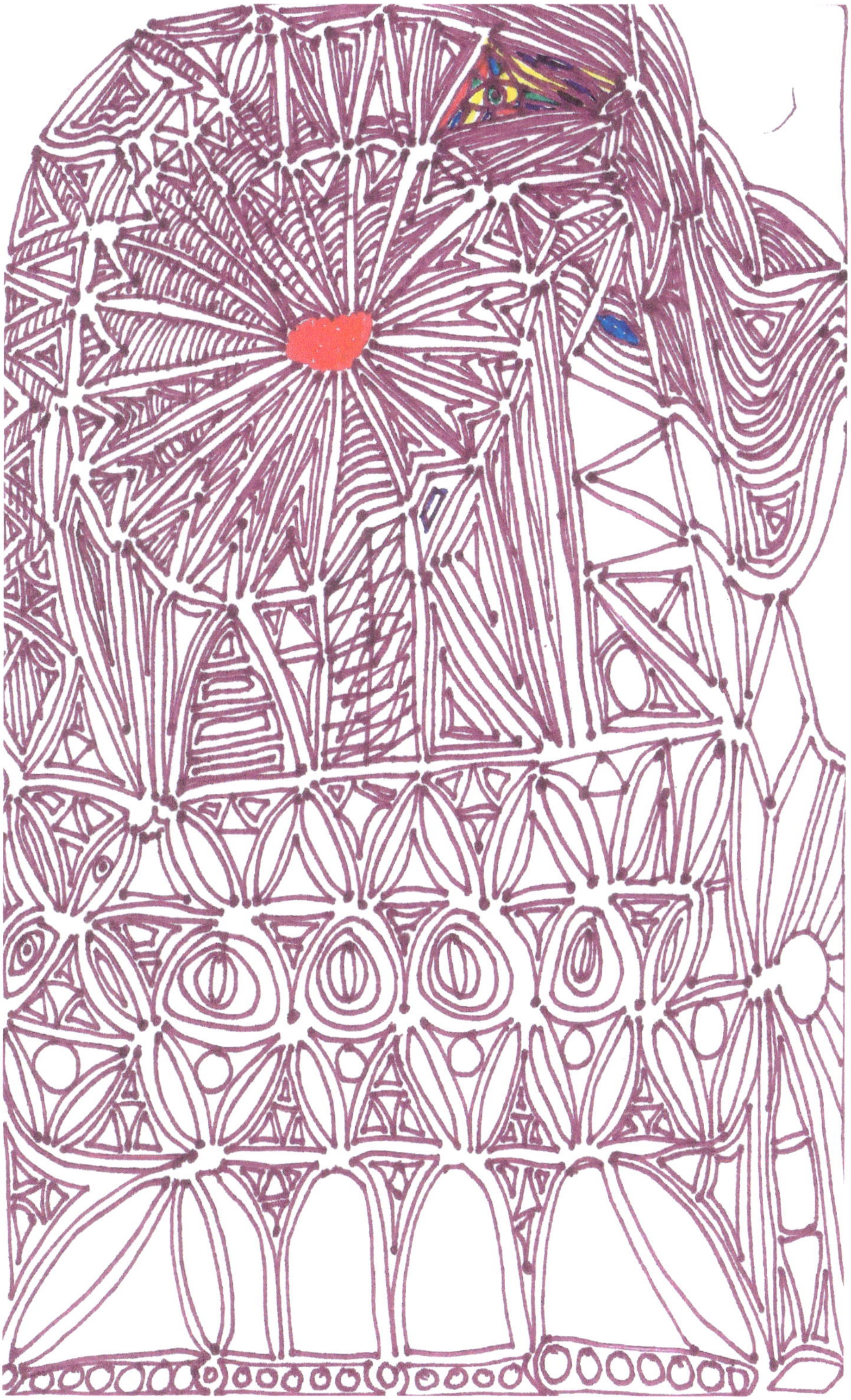

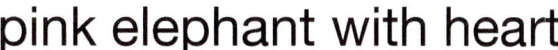

pink elephant with heart

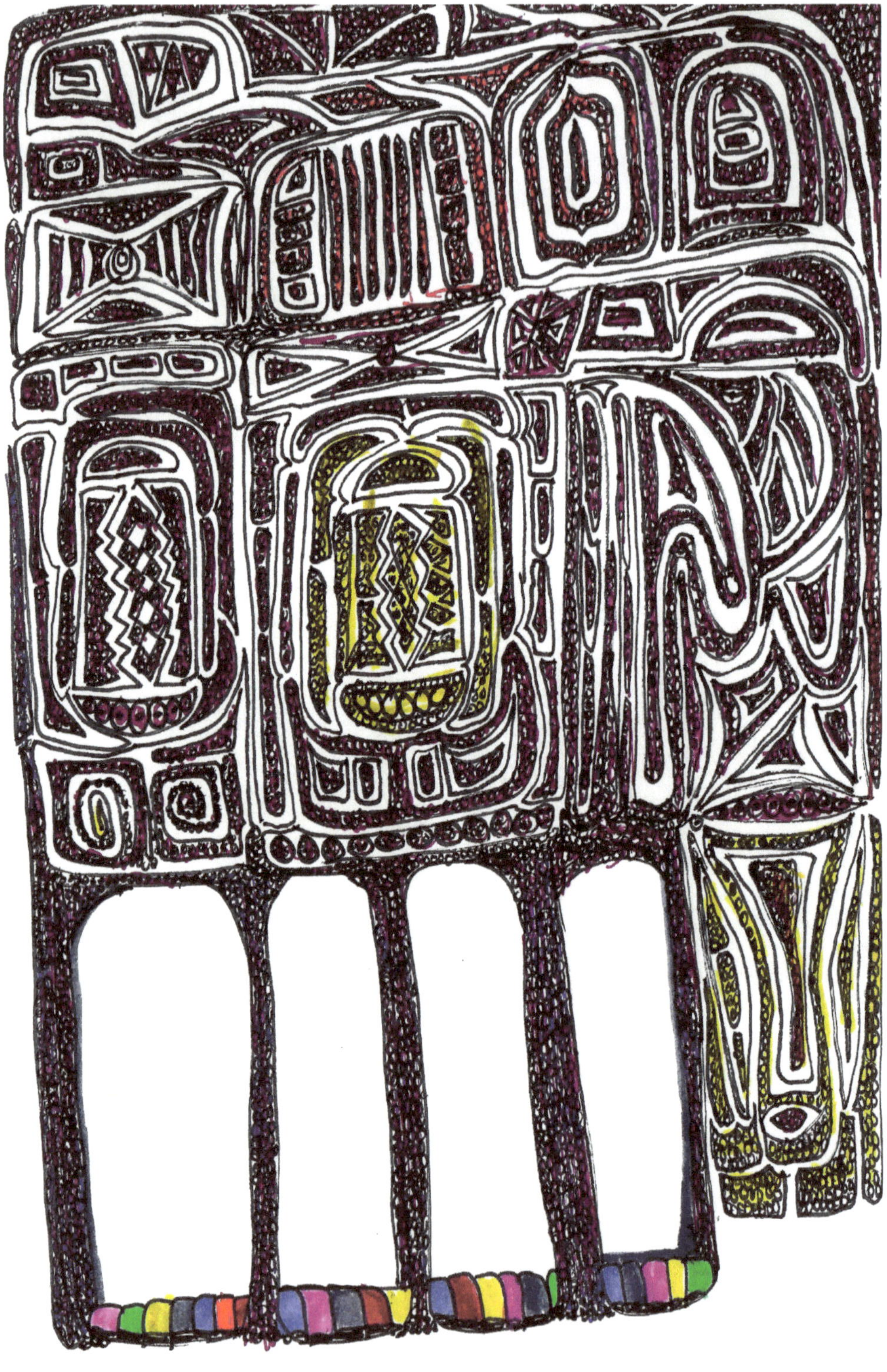

Daisy fled the nail salon in the throes of a panic attack. Her paralyzing indecision had become out of control.

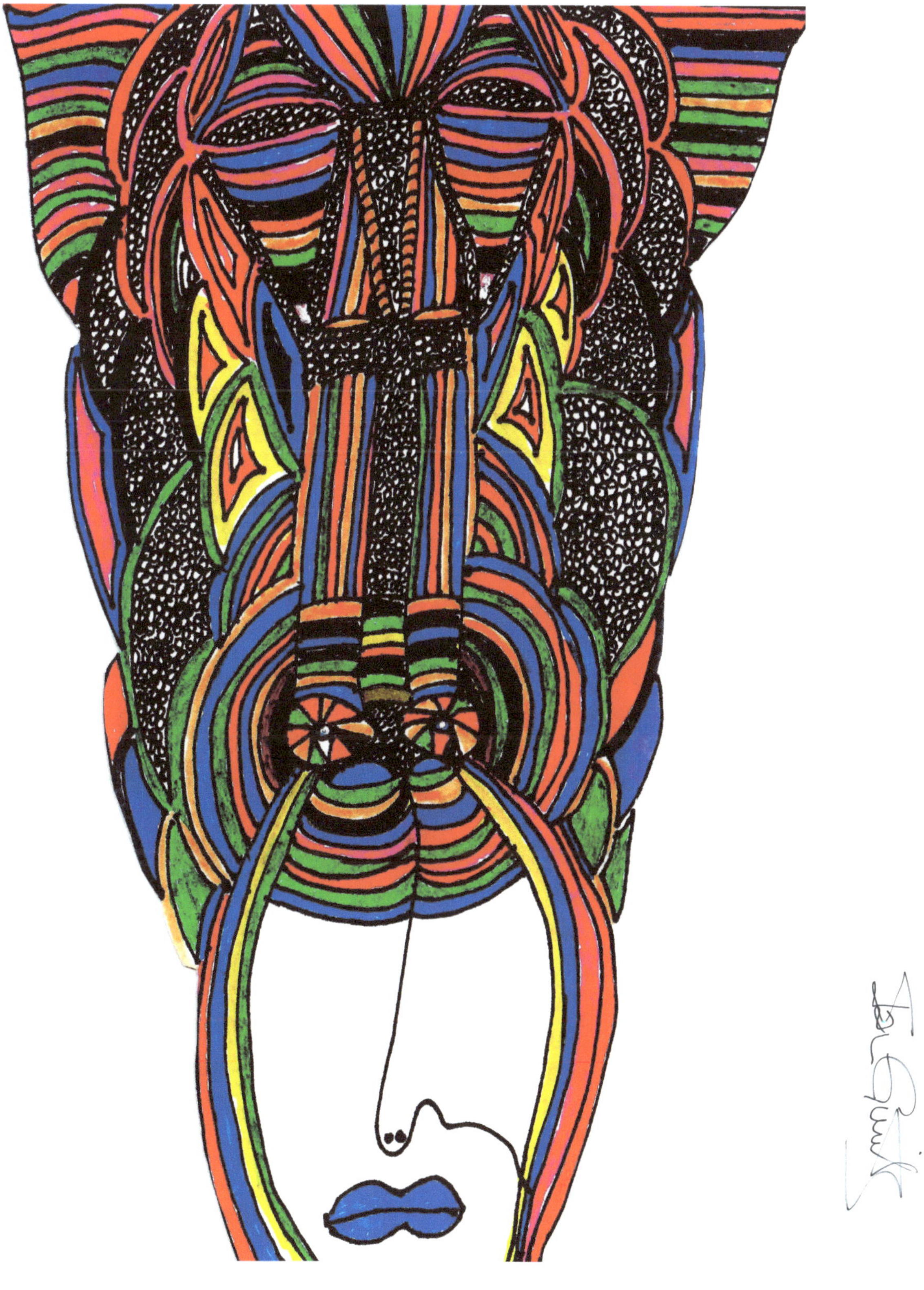

*demon or lady?*

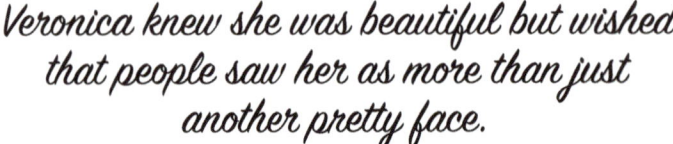

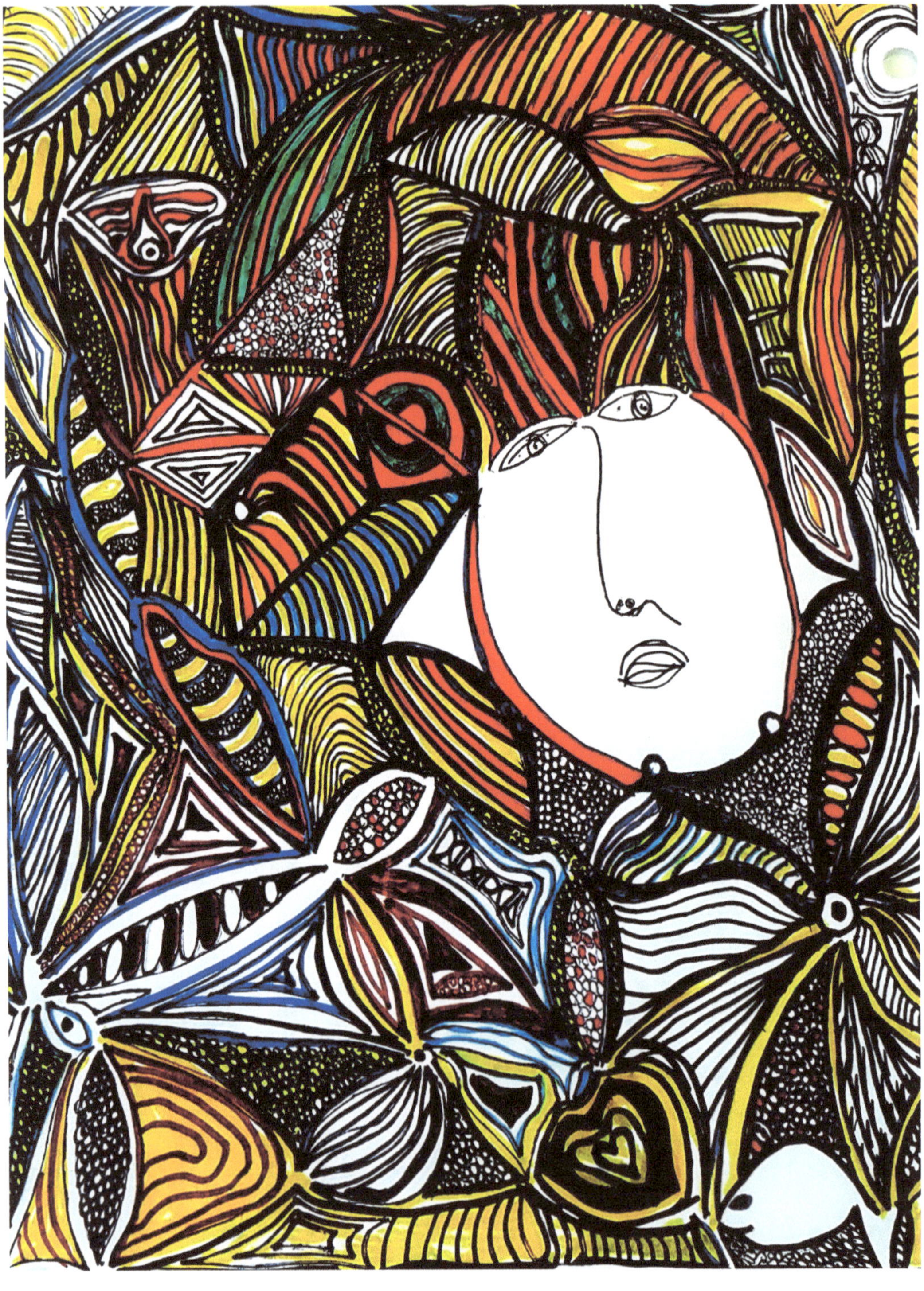

*Veronica knew she was beautiful but wished that people saw her as more than just another pretty face.*

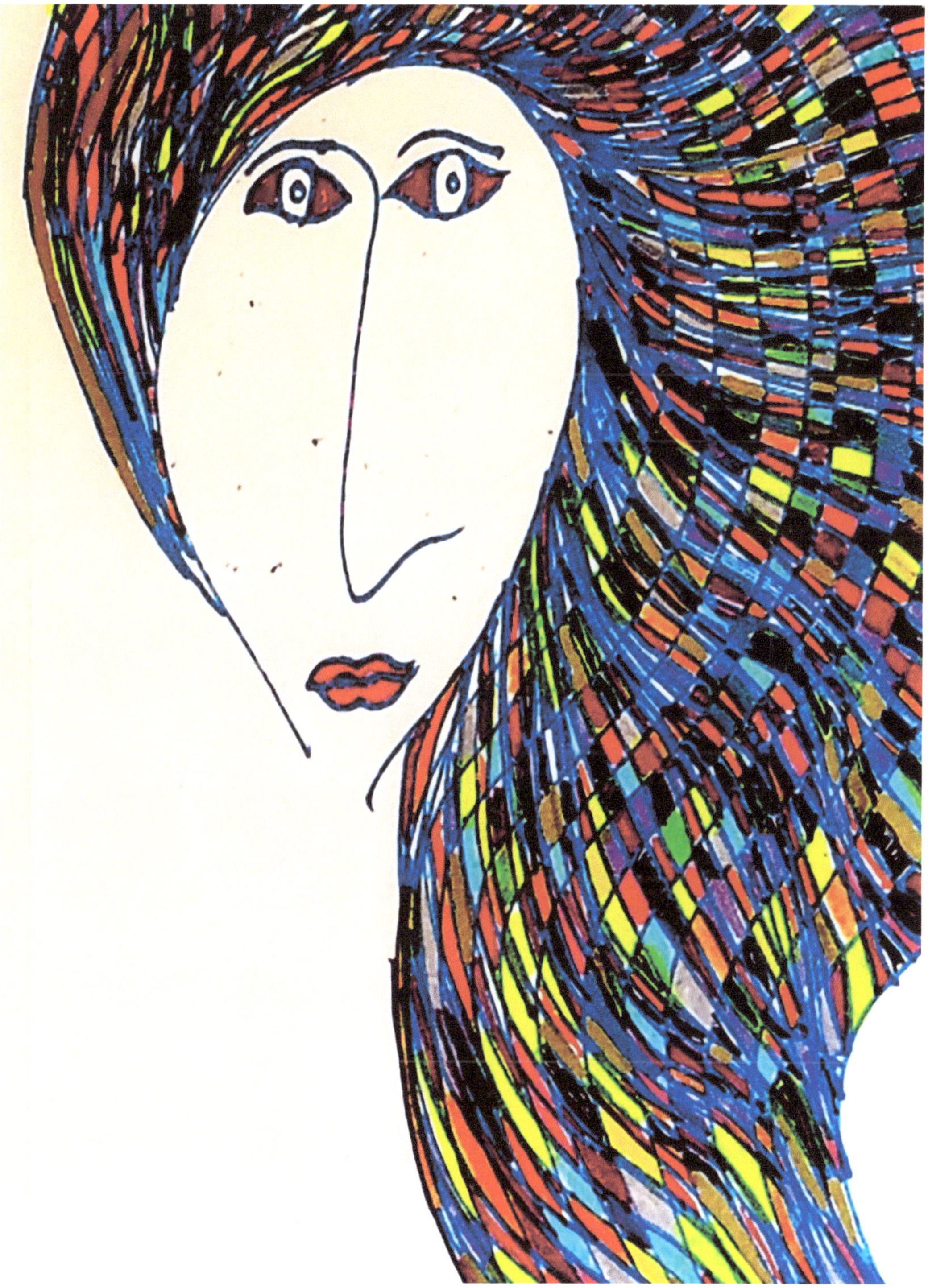

*the girl with kaleidoscope hair*

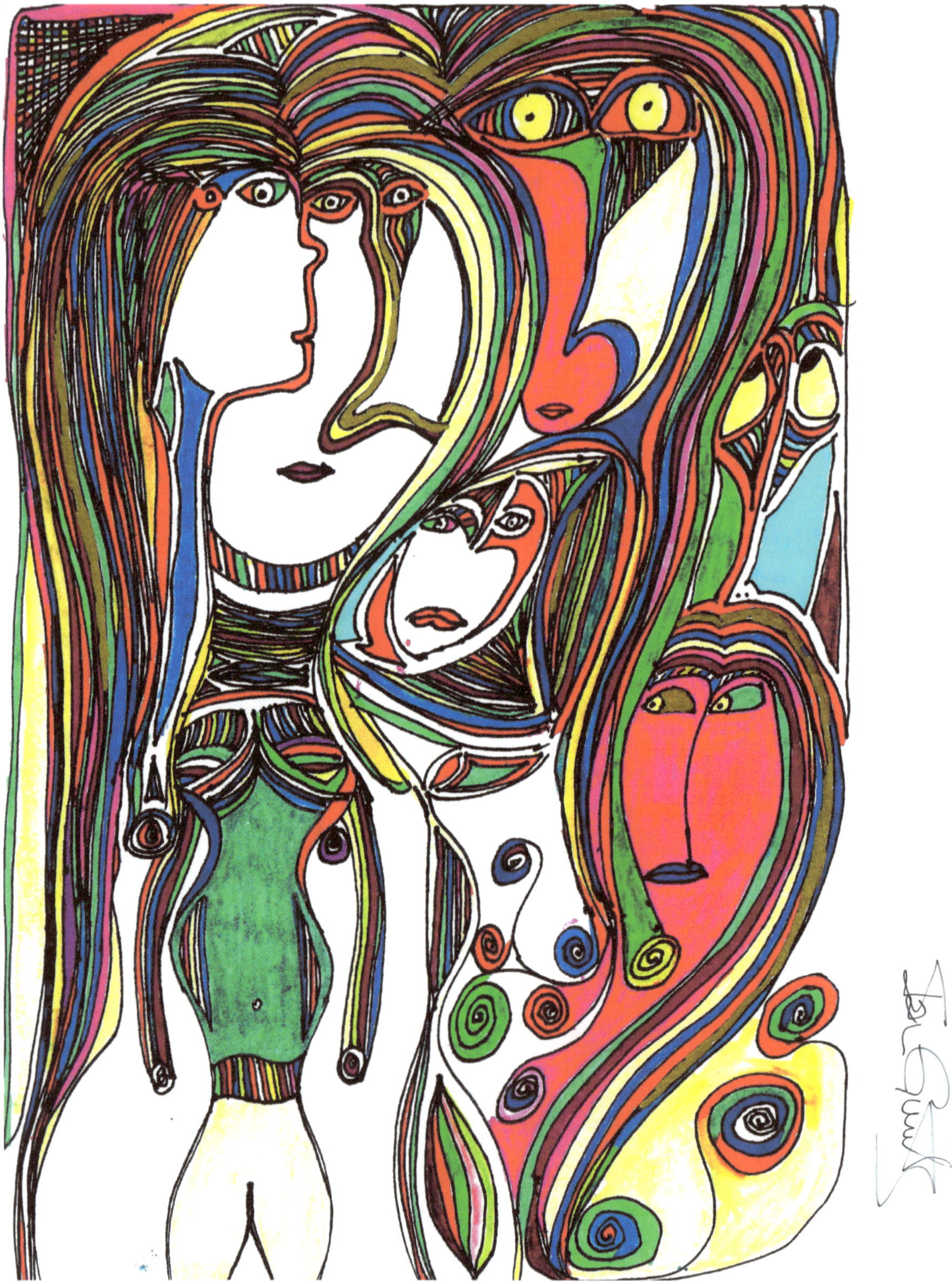

*girls' night out*

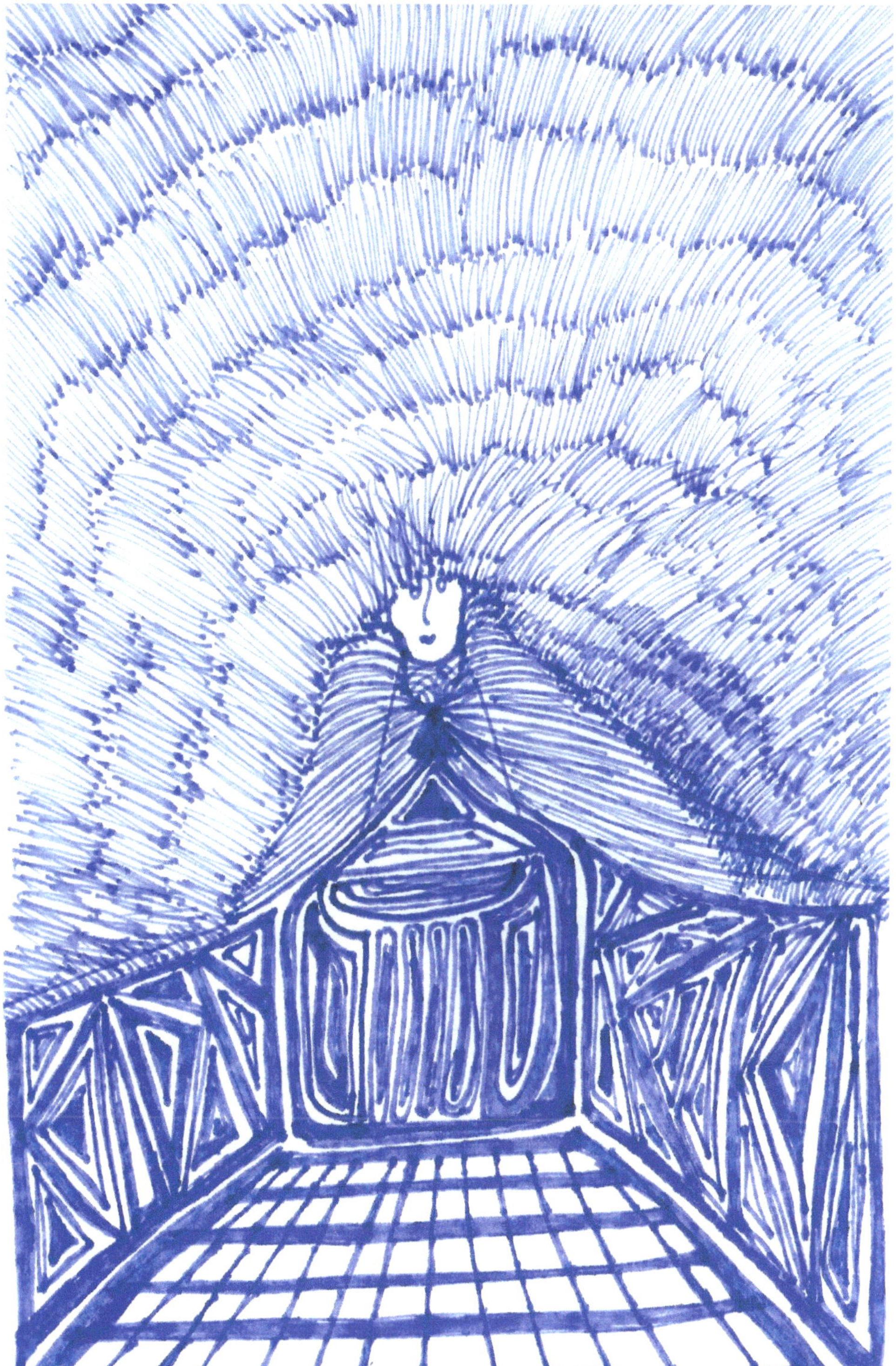

*Roxanne often dreamed she was back on stage in all her former glory.*

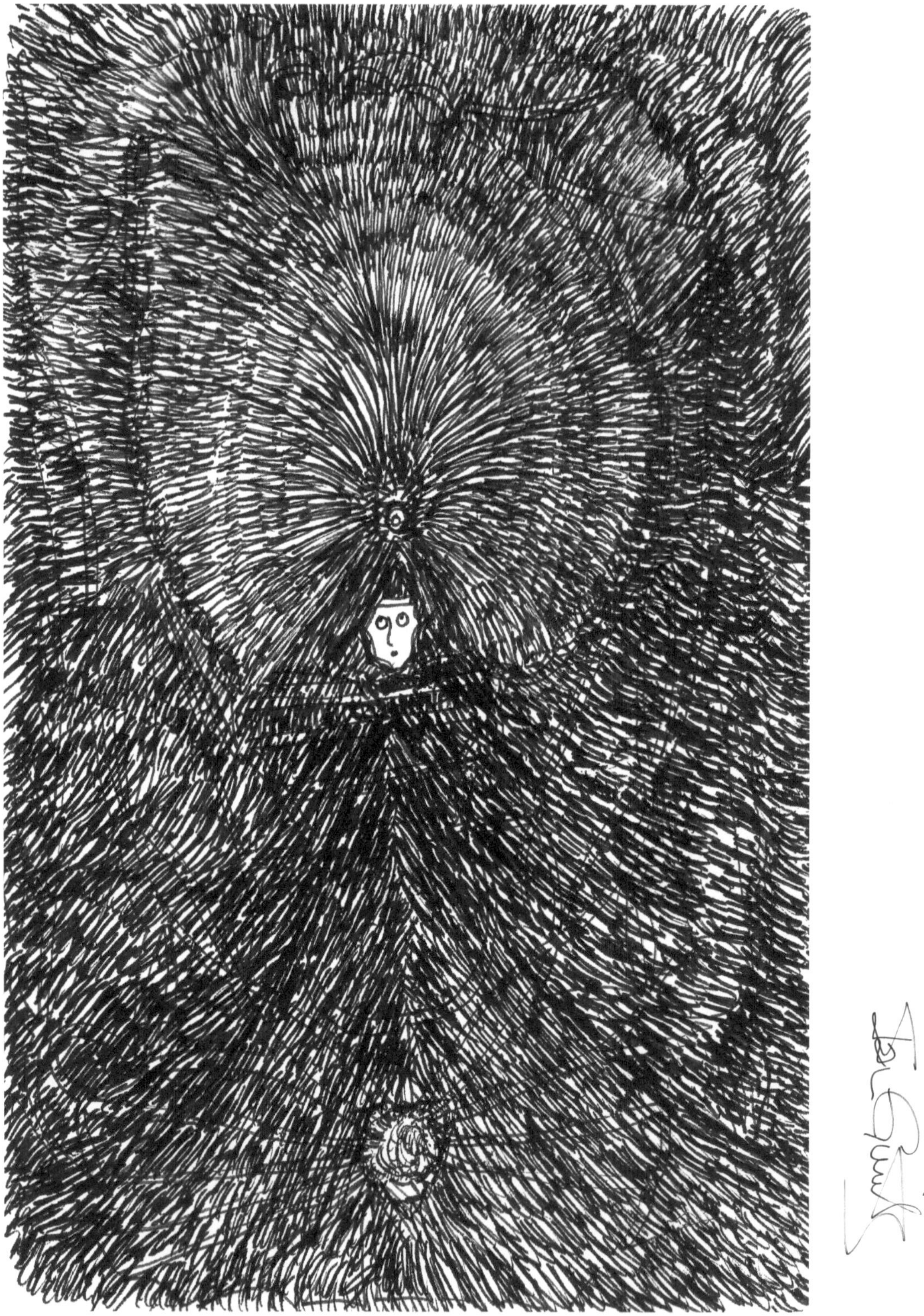

It slowly began to dawn on Brenda that her
perm was out of control.

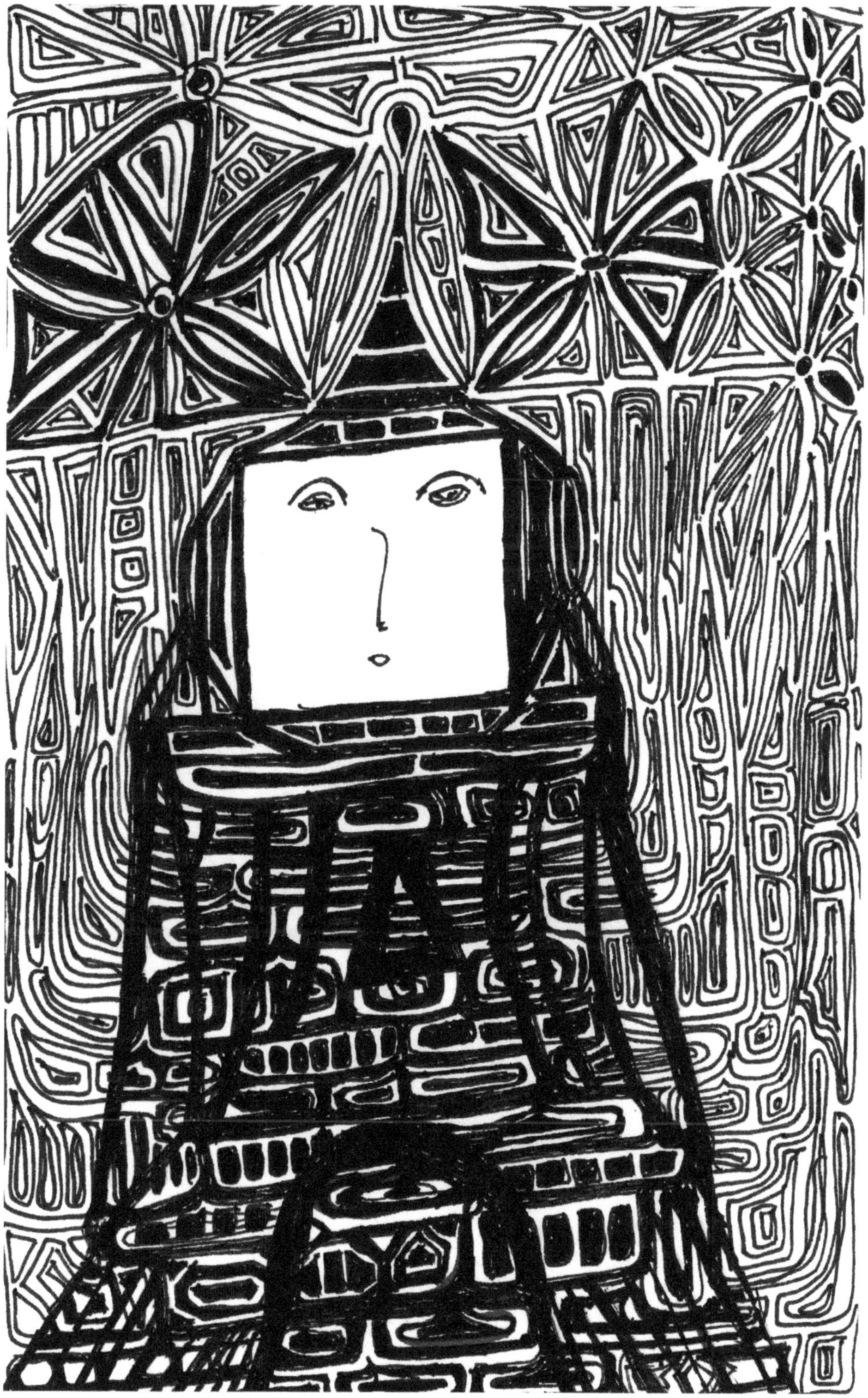

Trapped in her daily routine, Sheila feared she'd never realize her dream of seeing Paris.

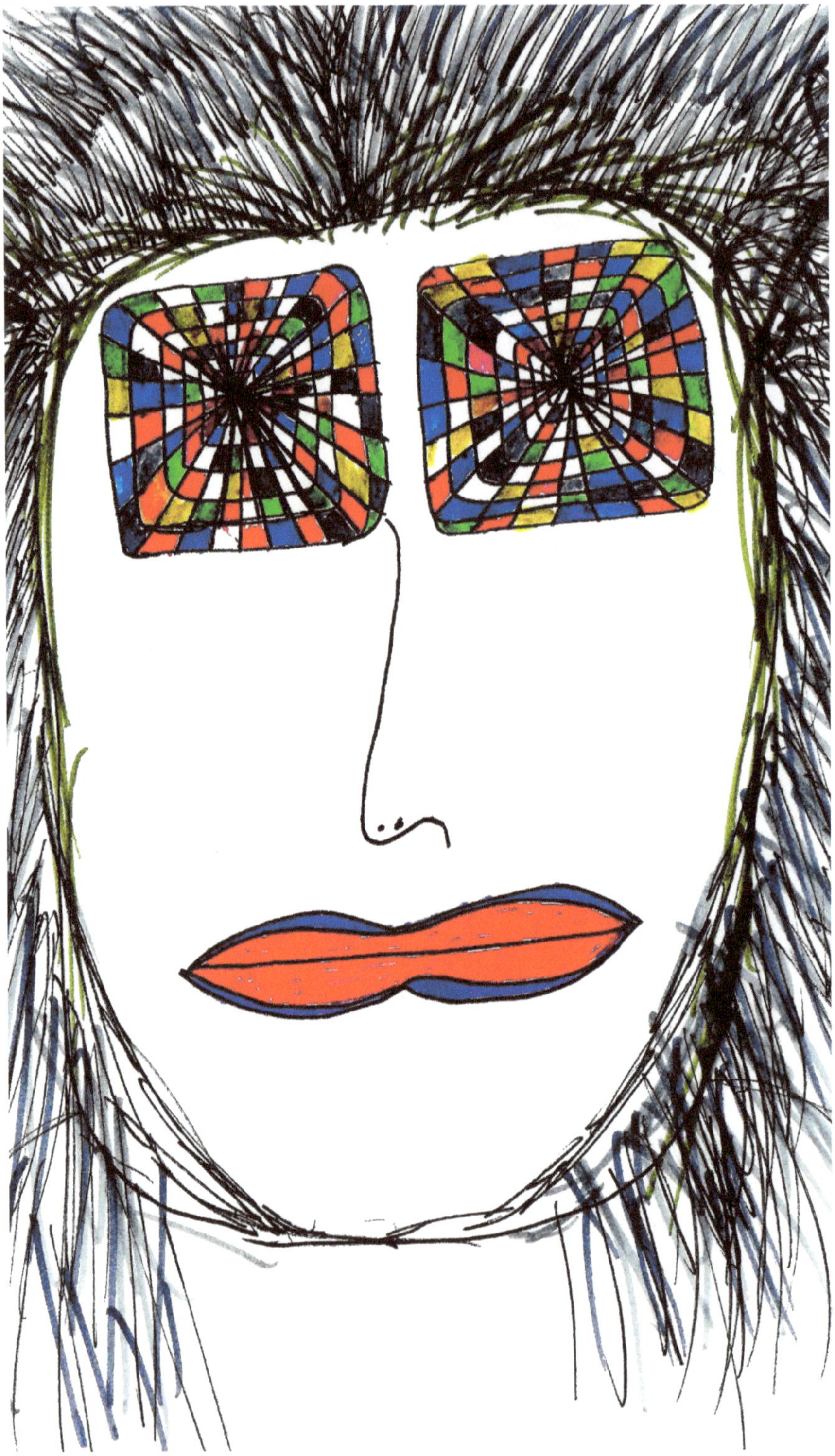

Nigel was excited about going back on the road, playing his hits for million of fans, yet privately he feared he was too burned out to survive another tour.

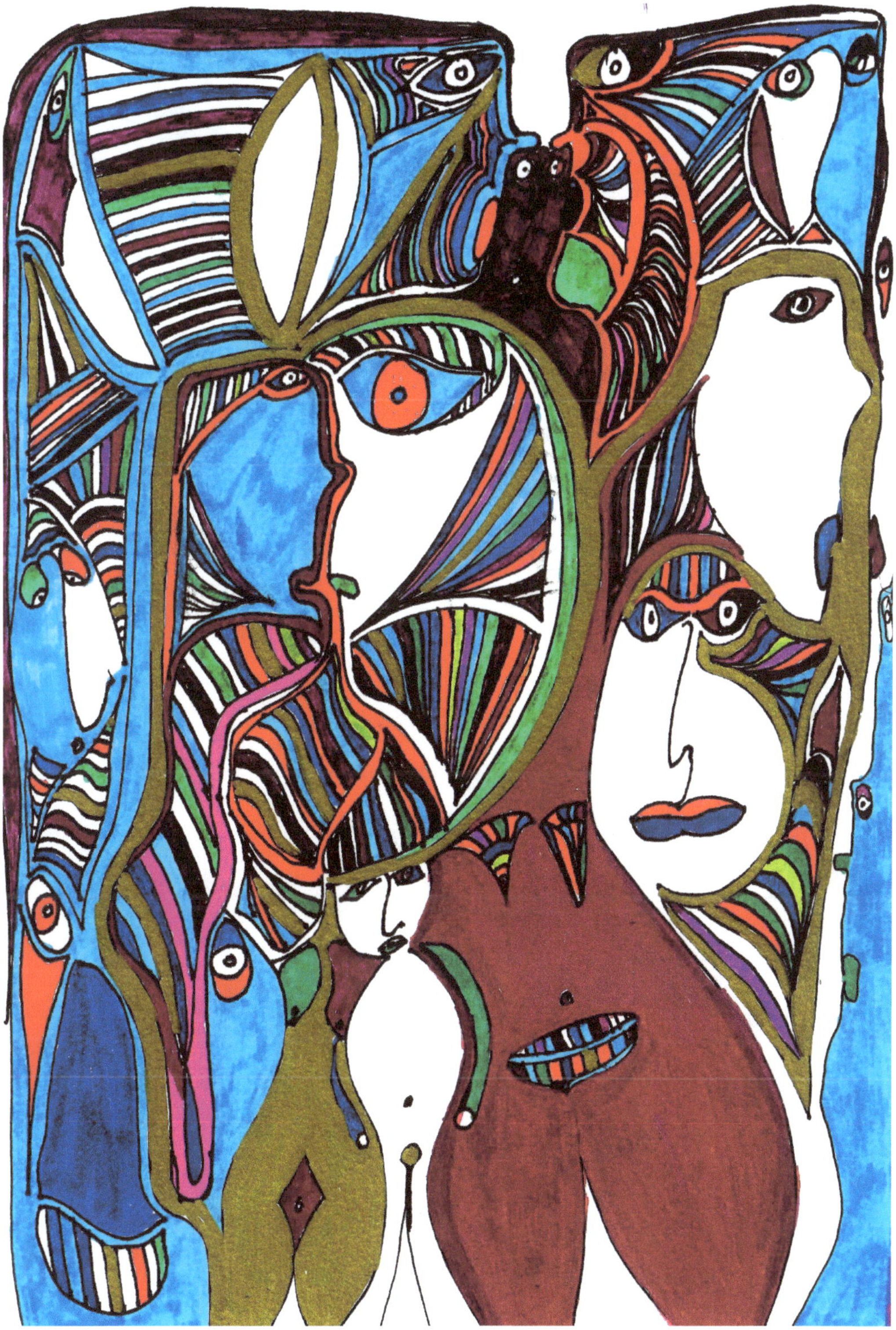

sex on the brain

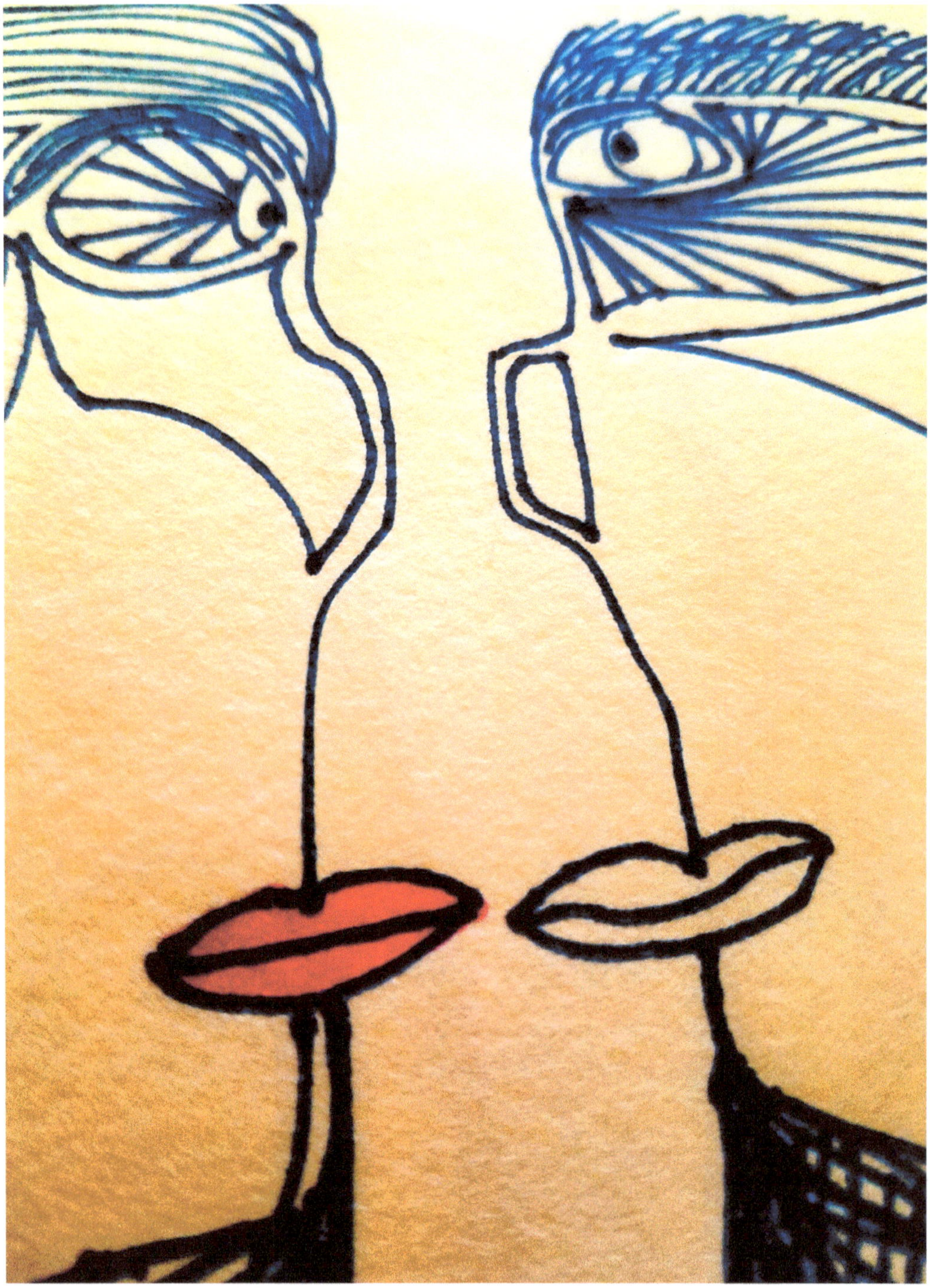

*kiss*

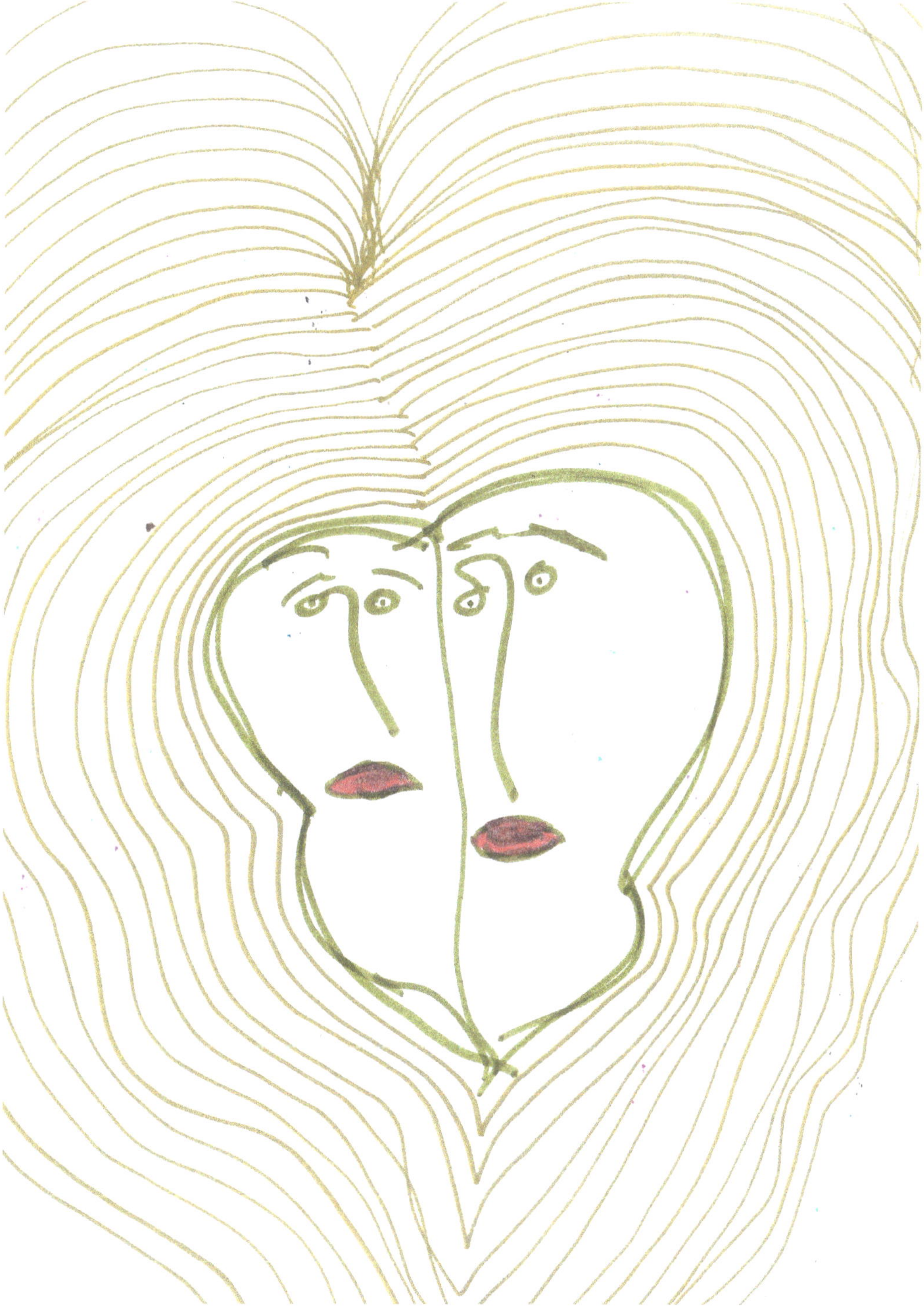

women in love

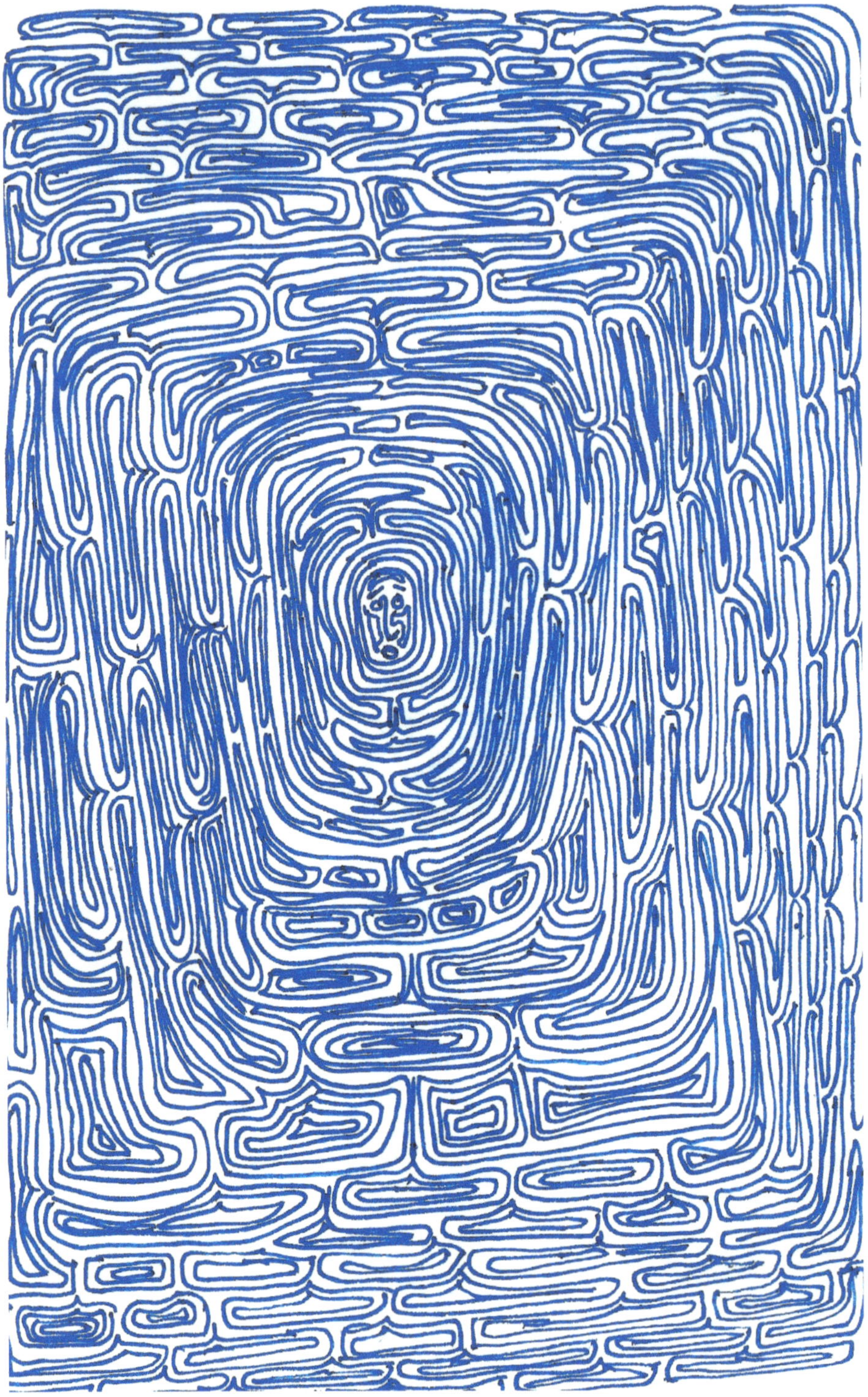

lost in the blues

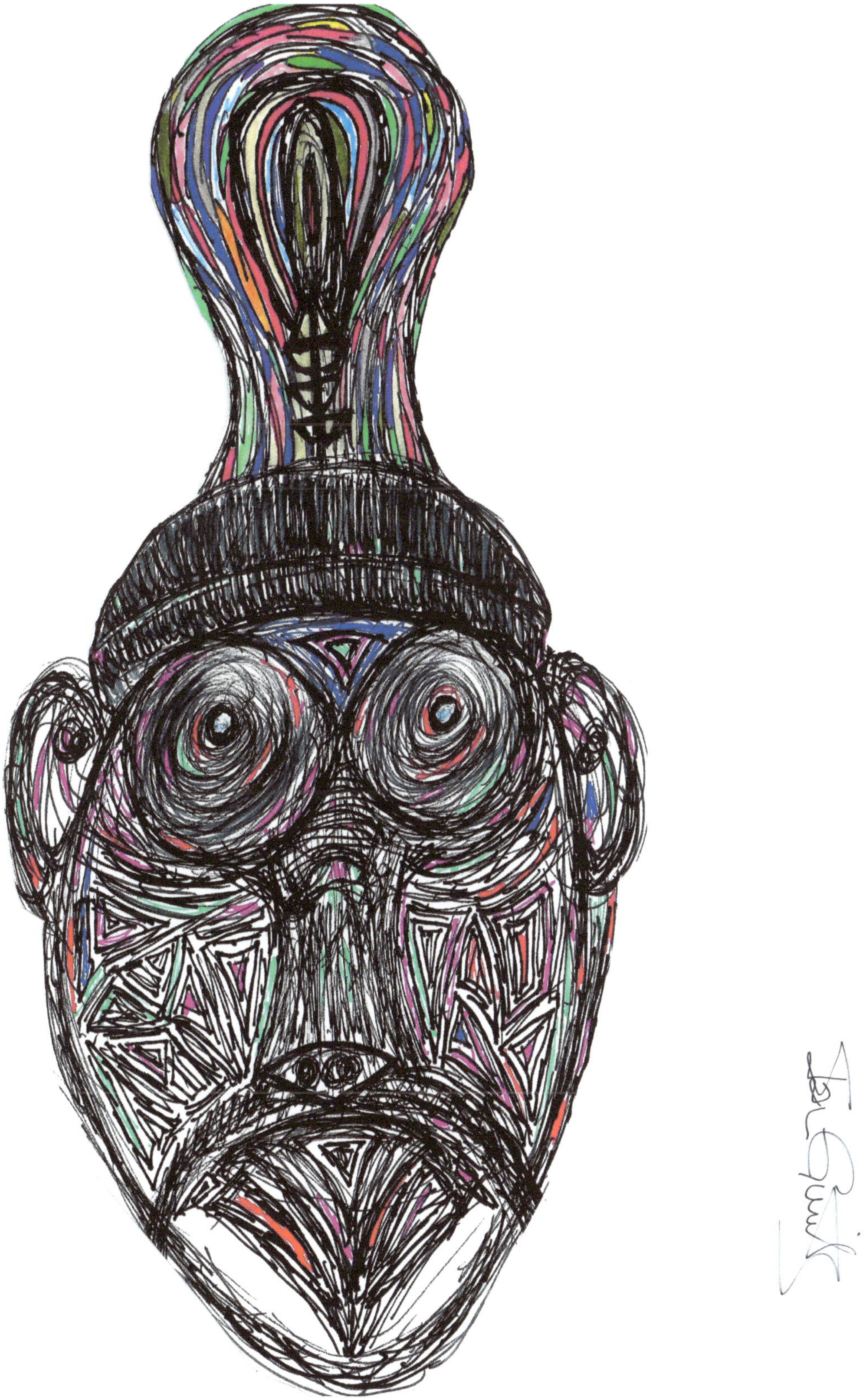

hipster with an idea

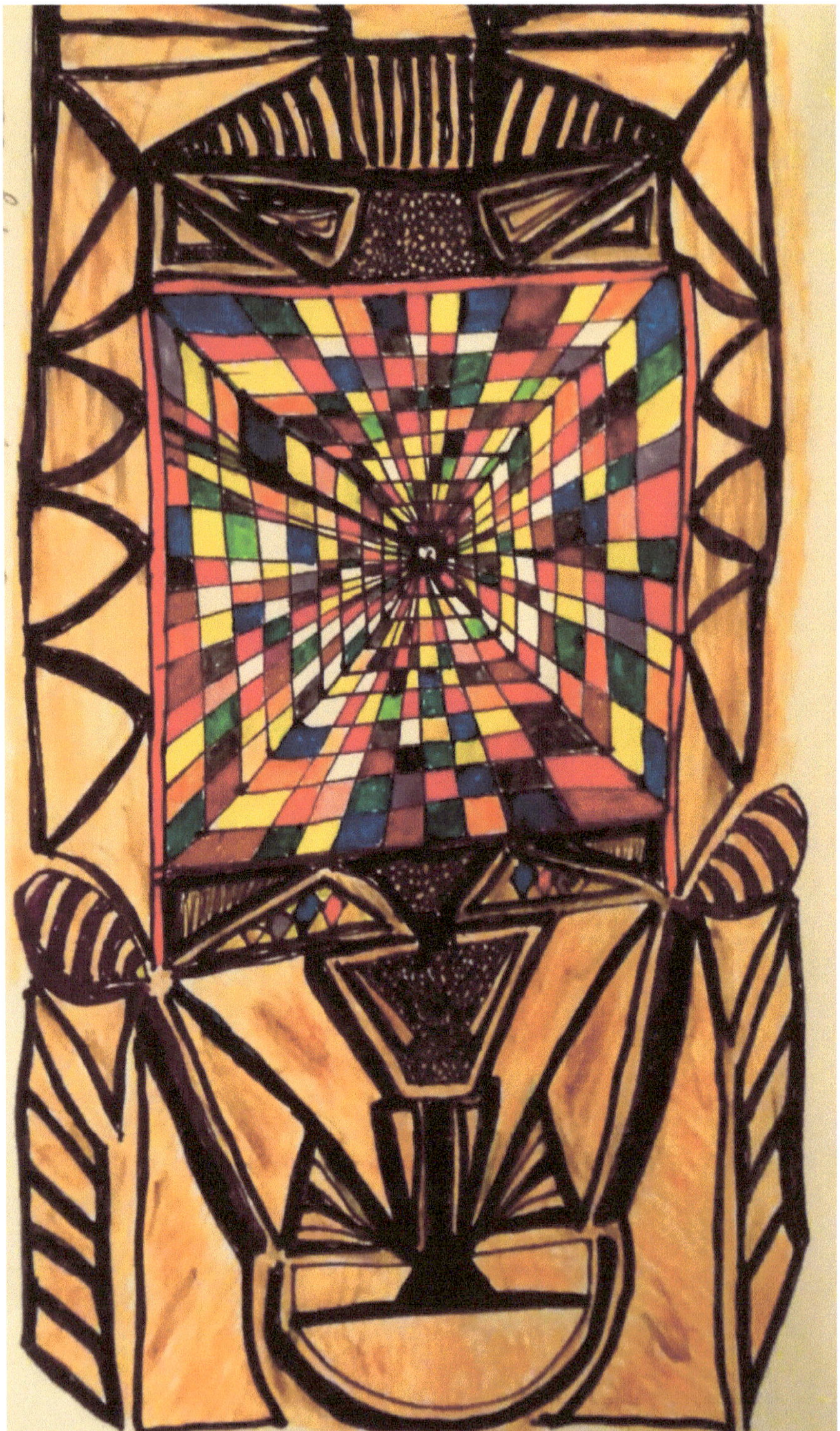

*dreams of a lion*

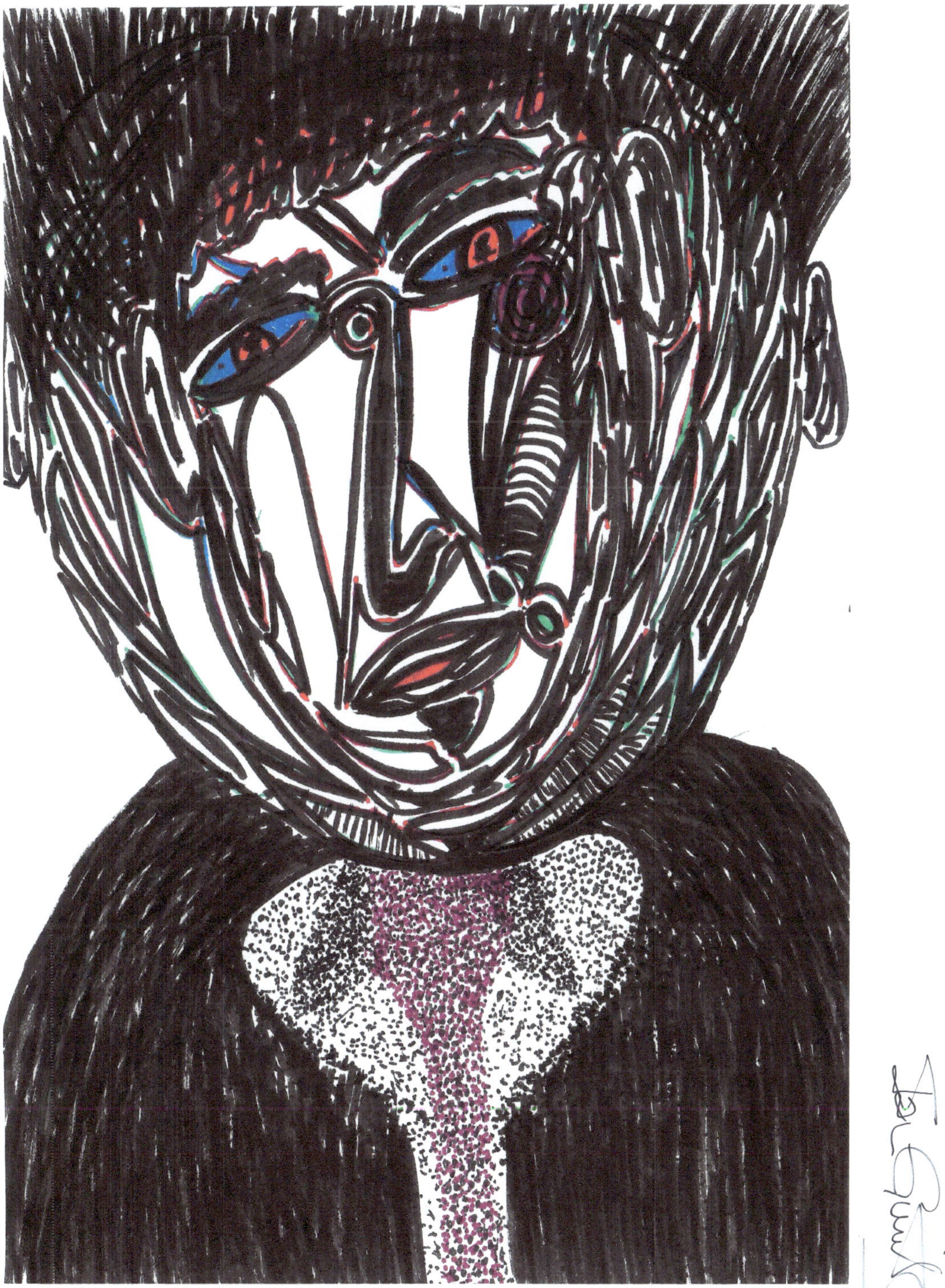

*Barclay stared in the mirror, feeling sadly conflicted. He regretted leaving his law practice behind, yet he was proud of being the first bear in his family to become a federal judge.*

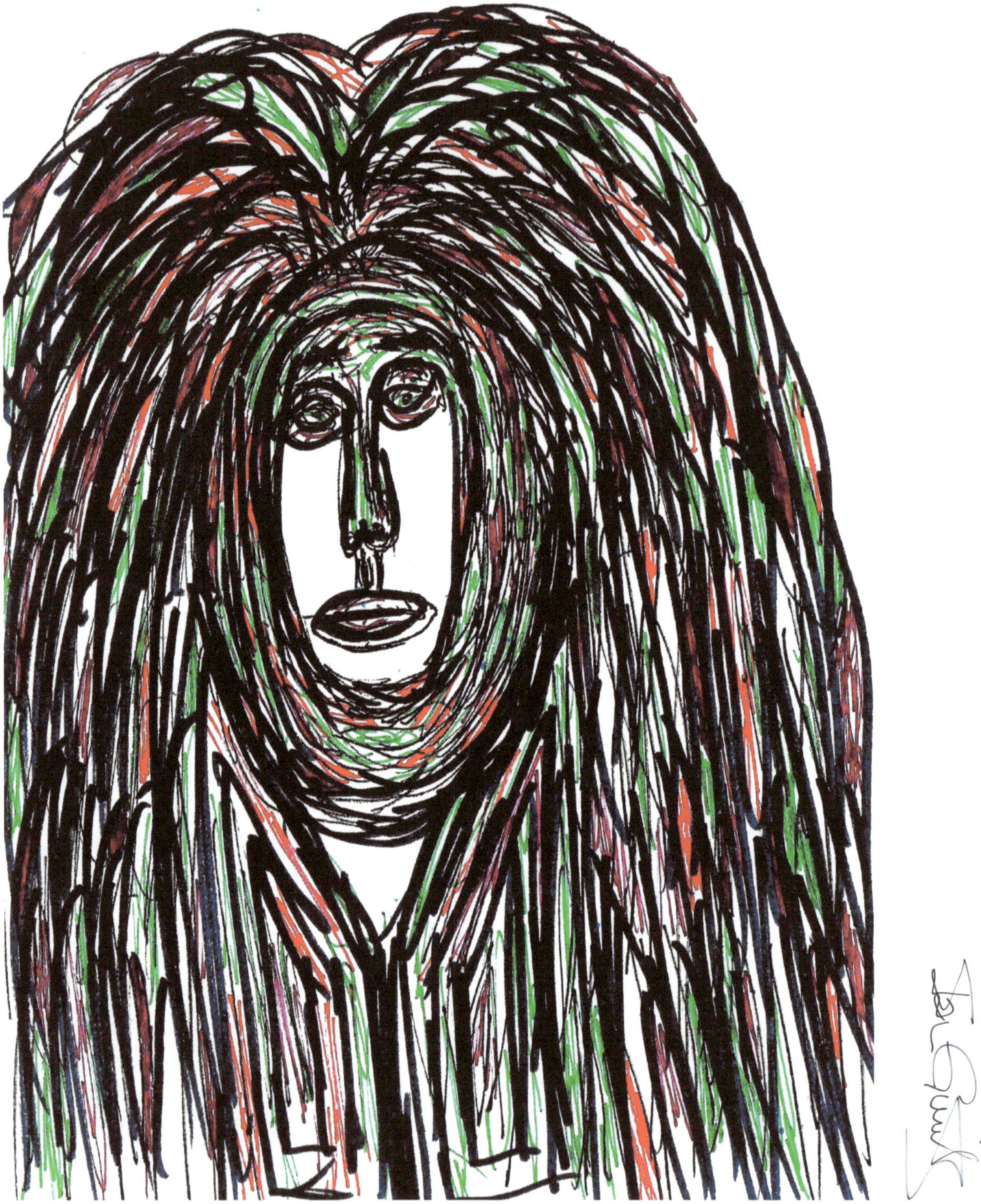

Rasta lion

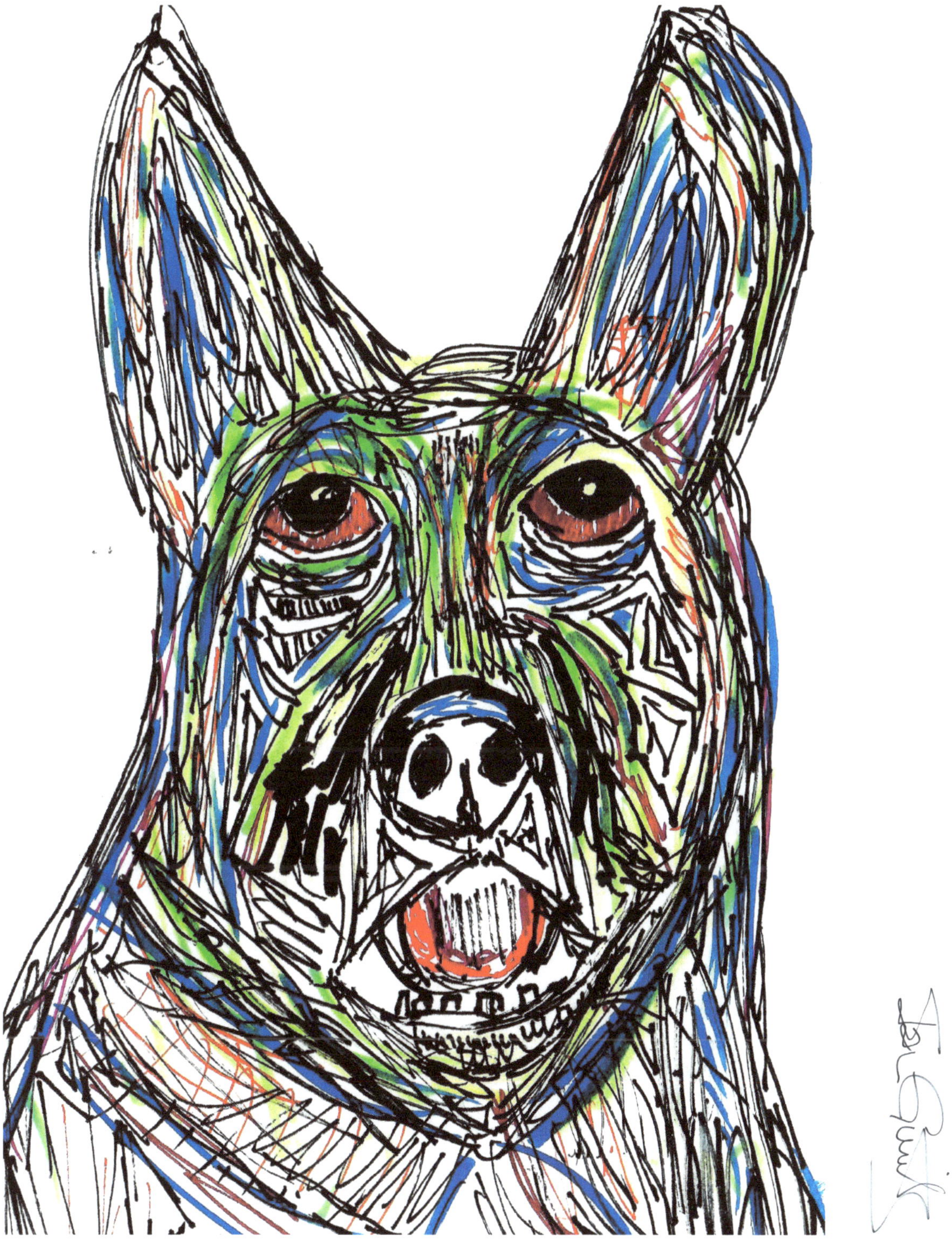

*And the prophet spoke unto the Dyslexics, saying: "I am the lord thy Dog! Thou shalt have no other Dogs before me!"*

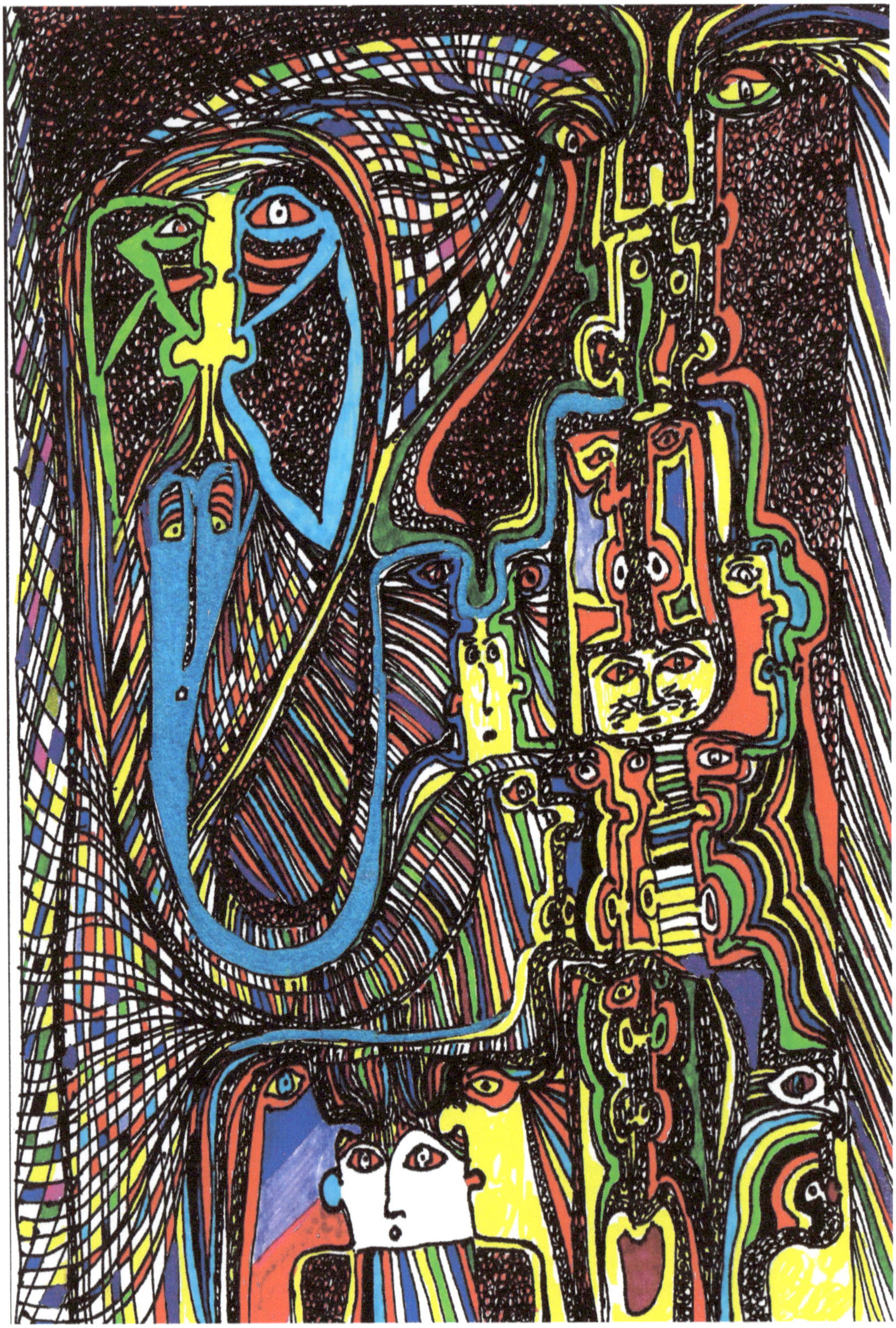

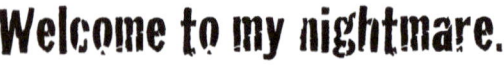

Welcome to my nightmare.

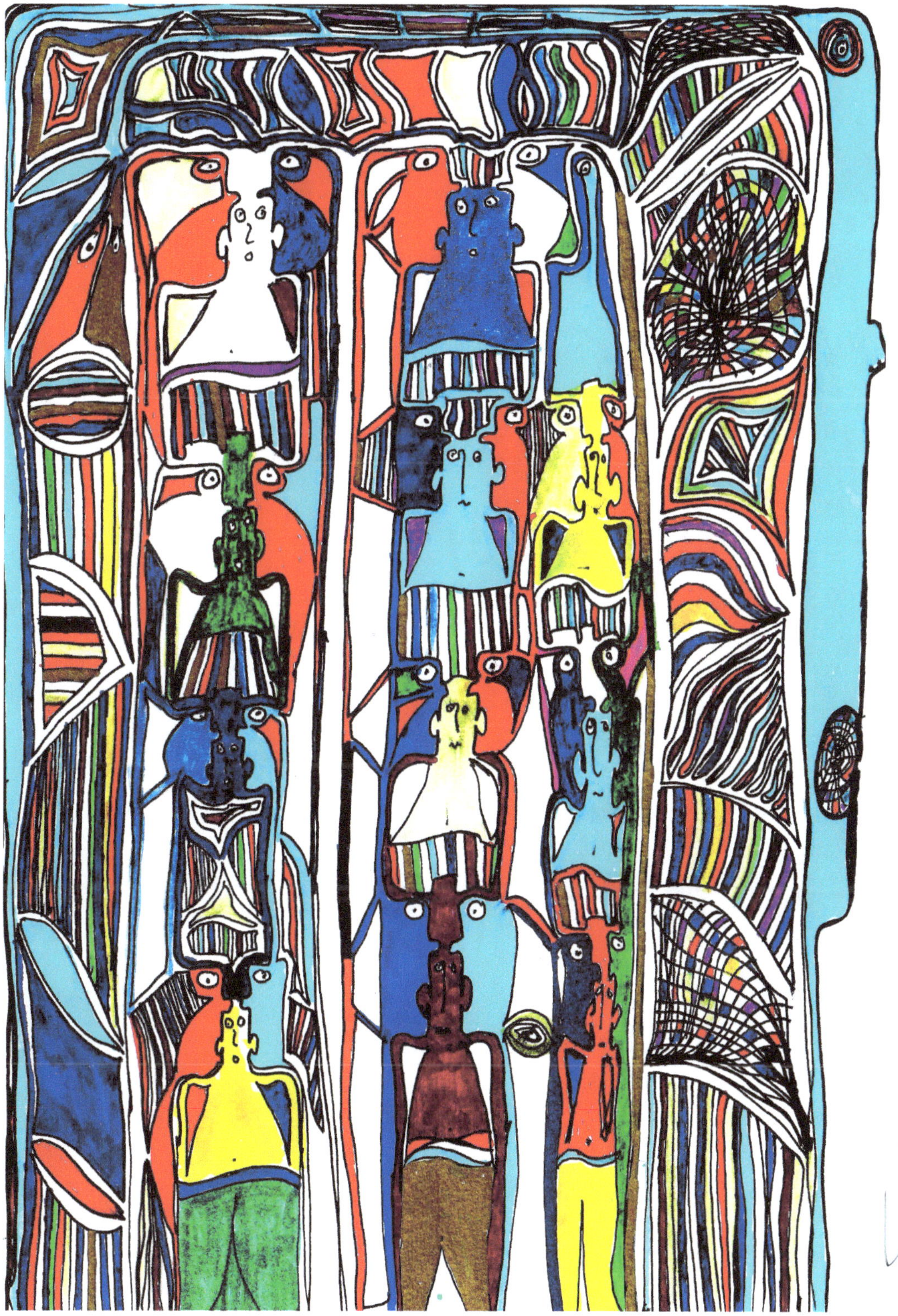

Try as he might, John couldn't silence
the voices in his head.

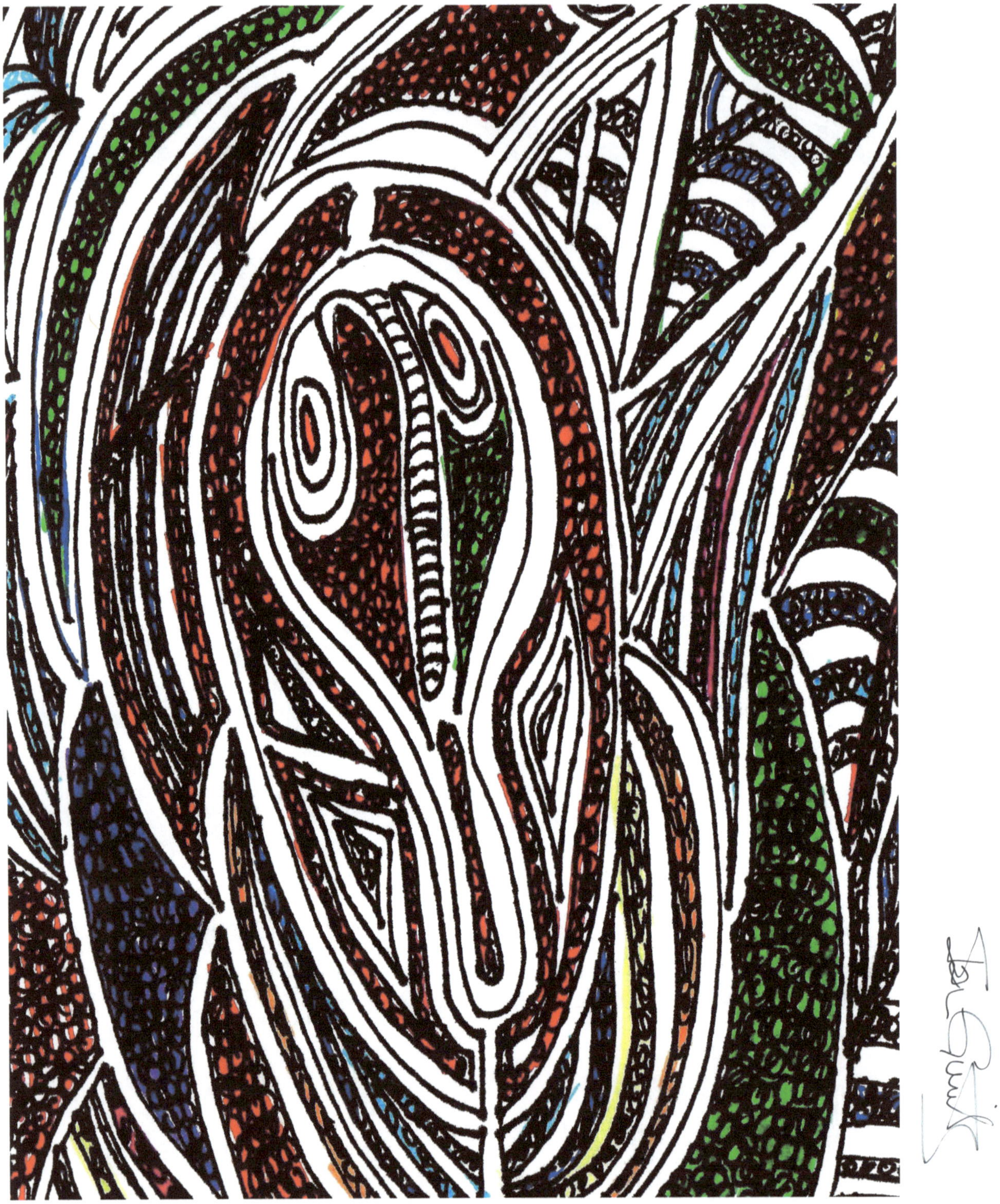

dream scream

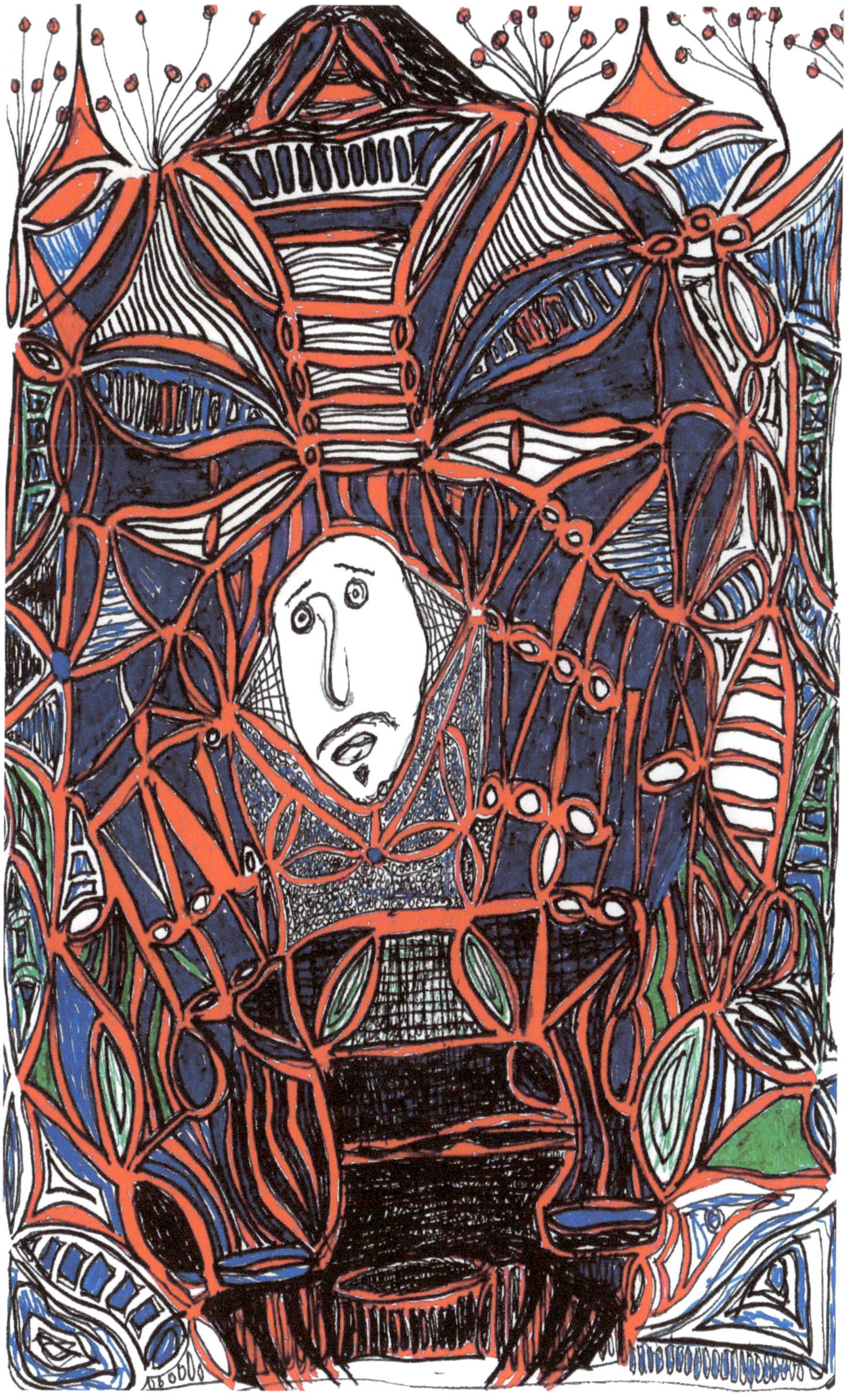

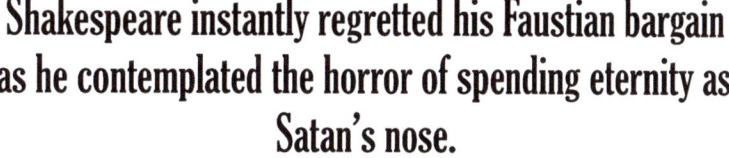

Shakespeare instantly regretted his Faustian bargain as he contemplated the horror of spending eternity as Satan's nose.

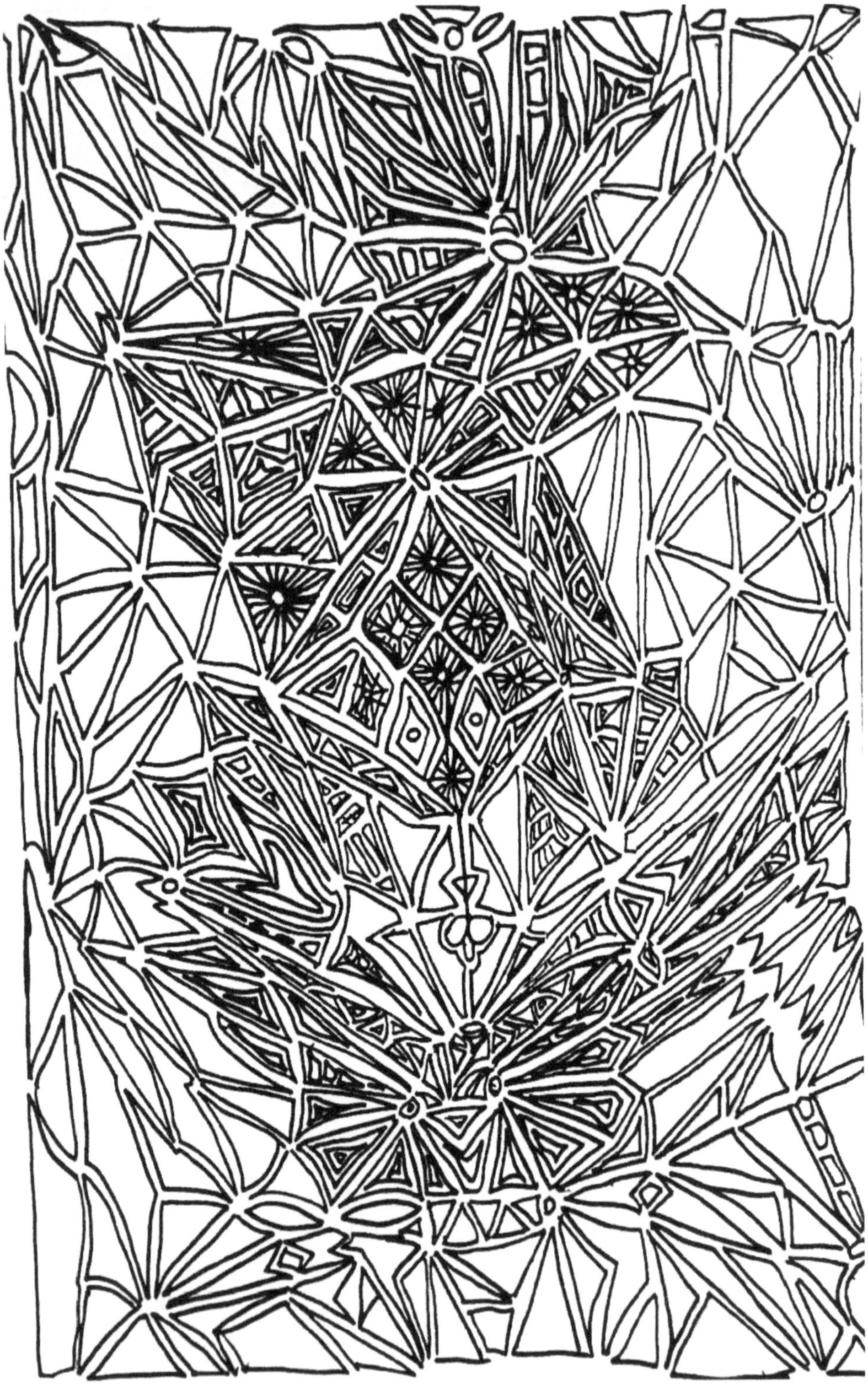

tweeky bunny

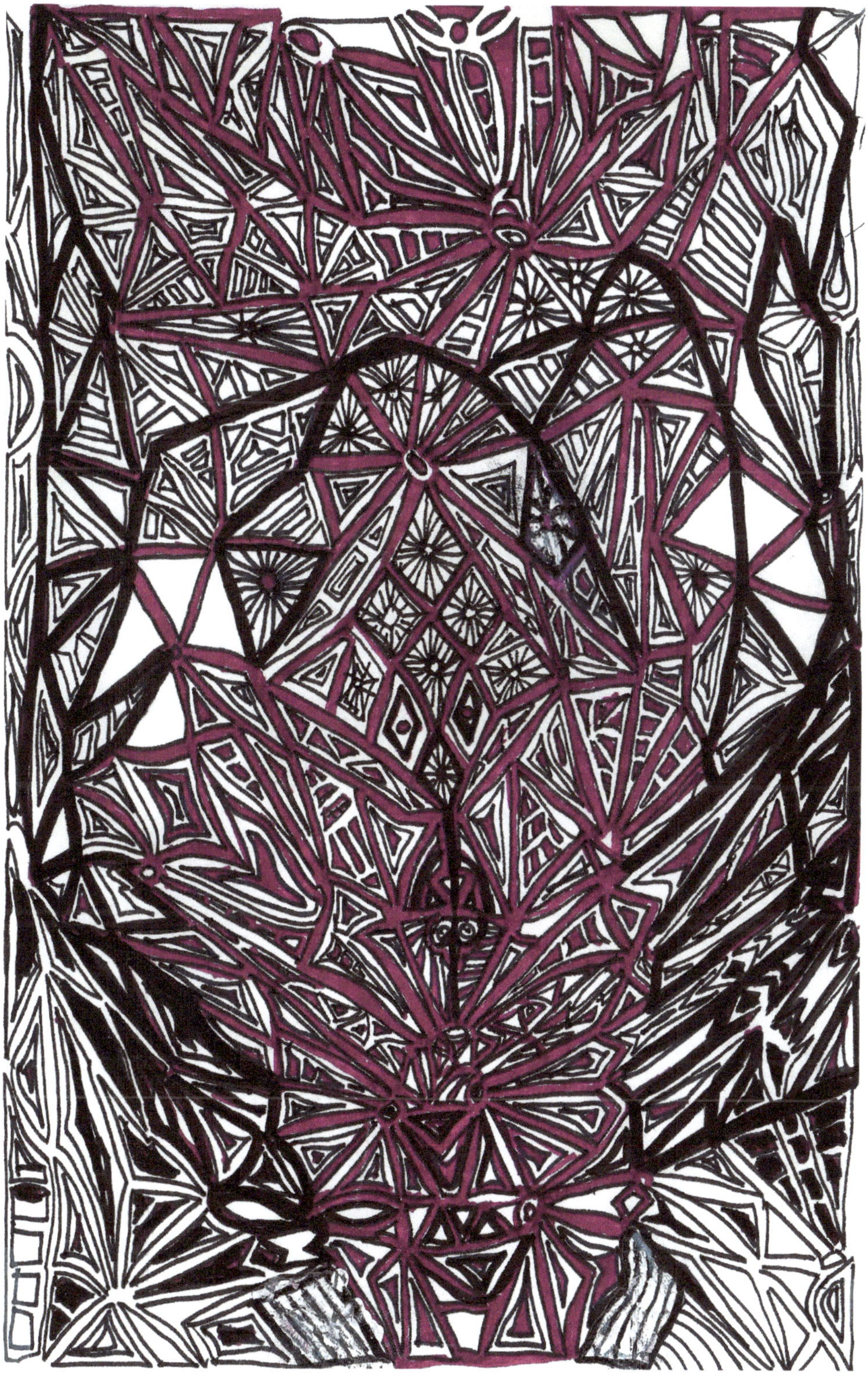

Fox eats tweeky bunny

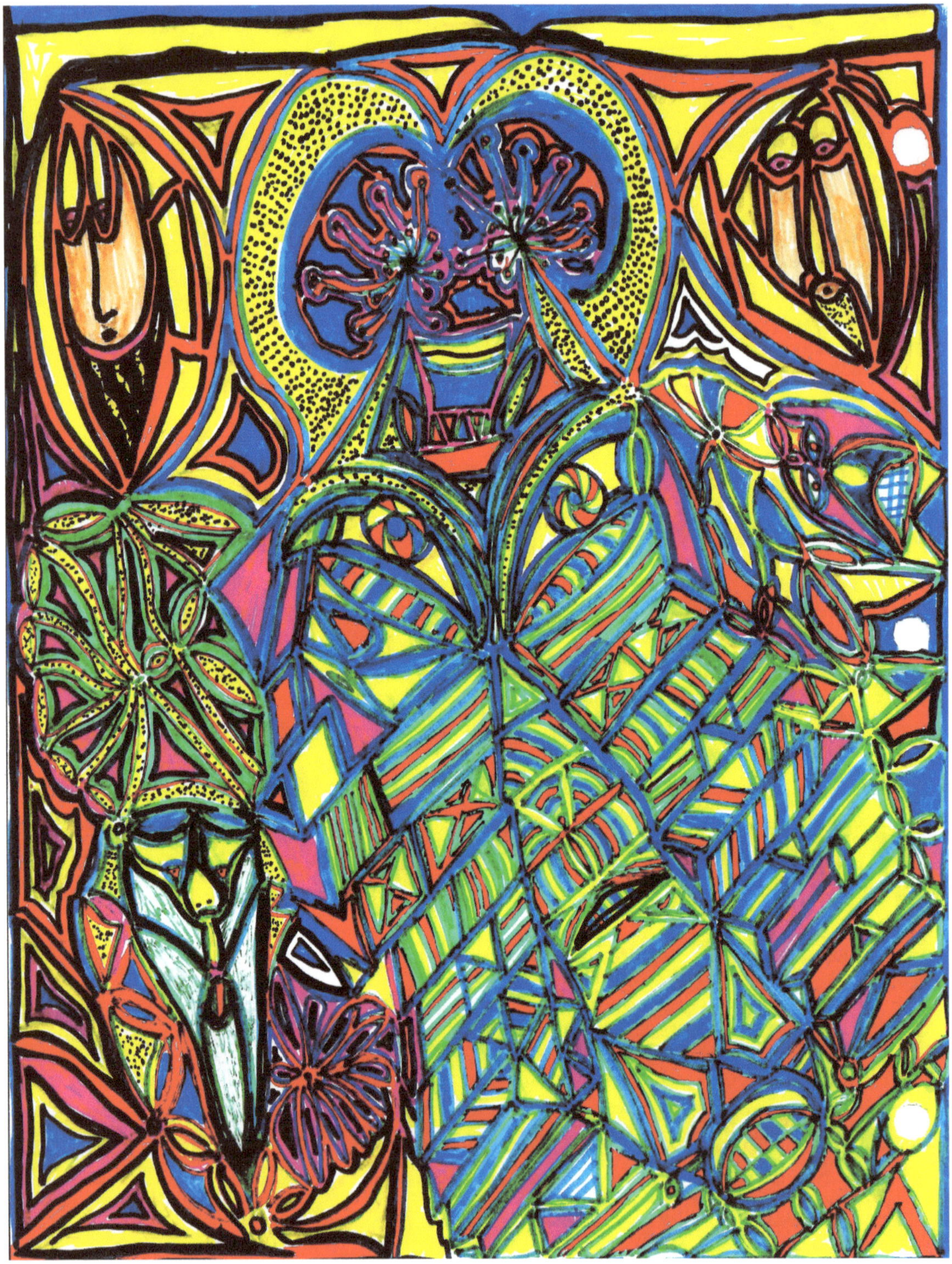

This is your drugs on brain.

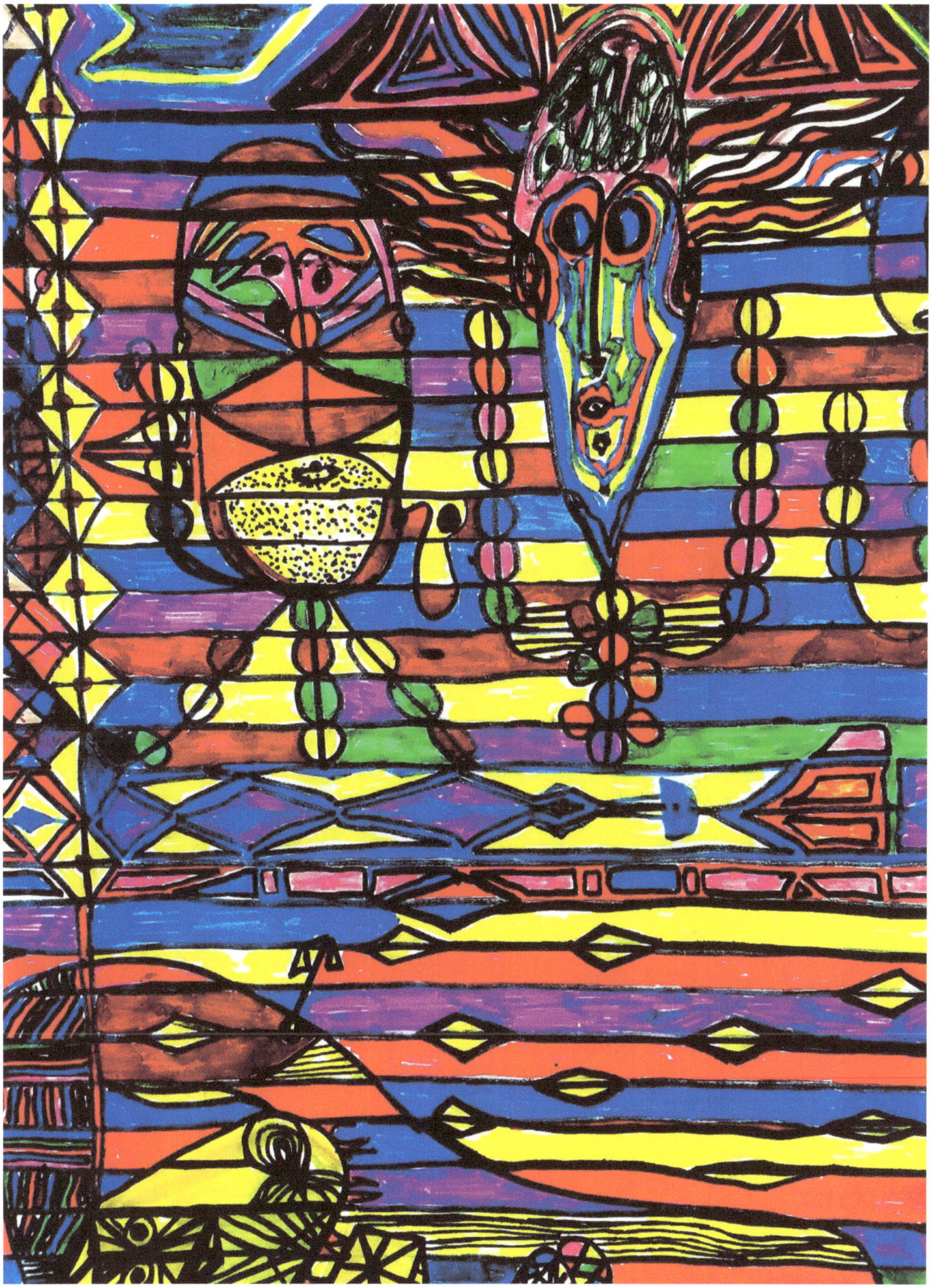

Moe and Larry blamed Curly for
scoring the bad acid.

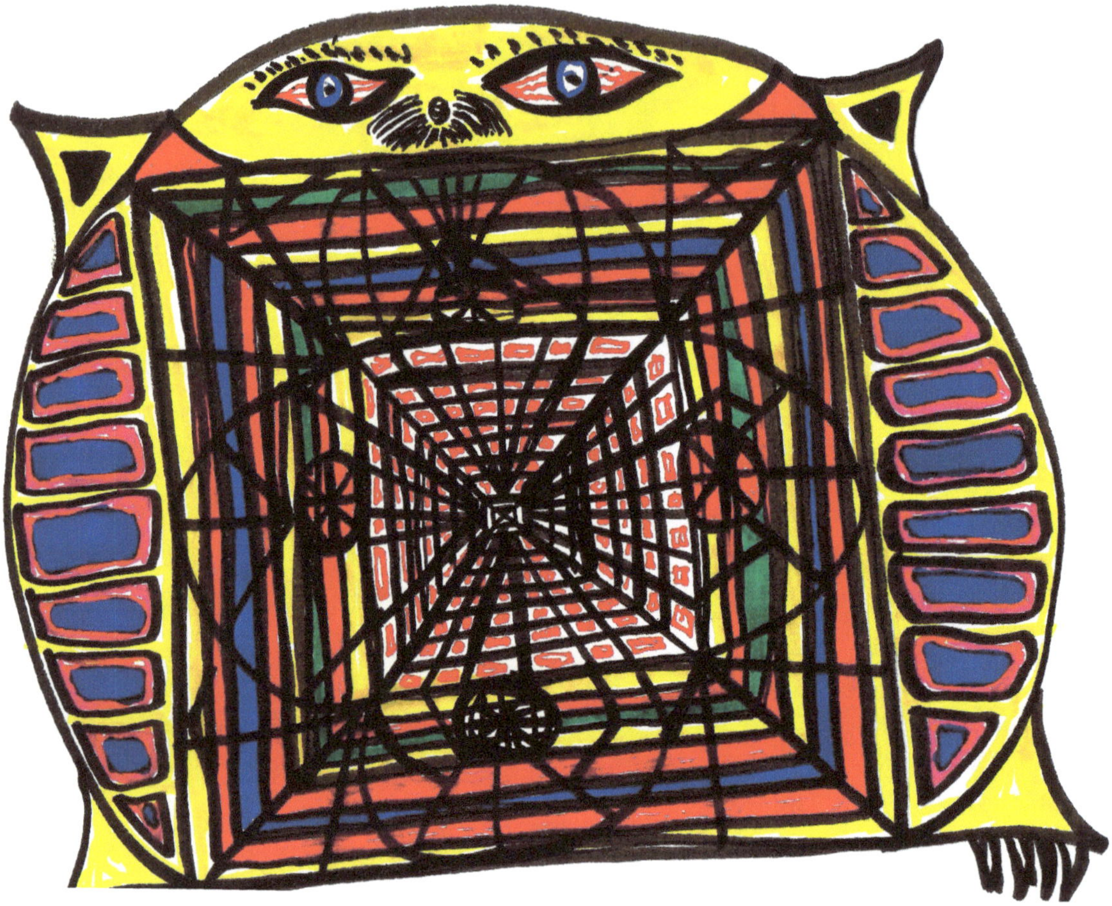

psychedelicat

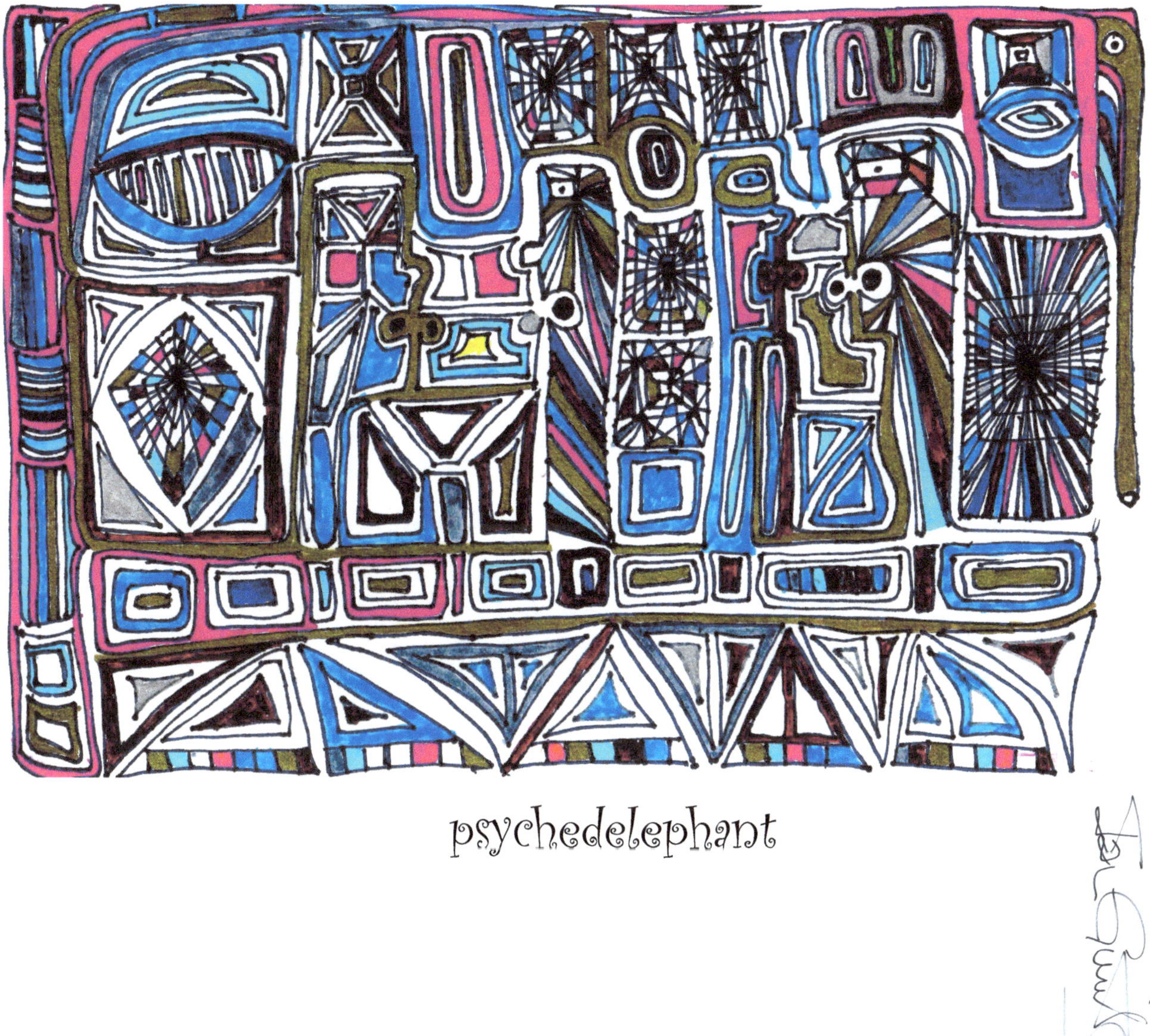

psychedelephant

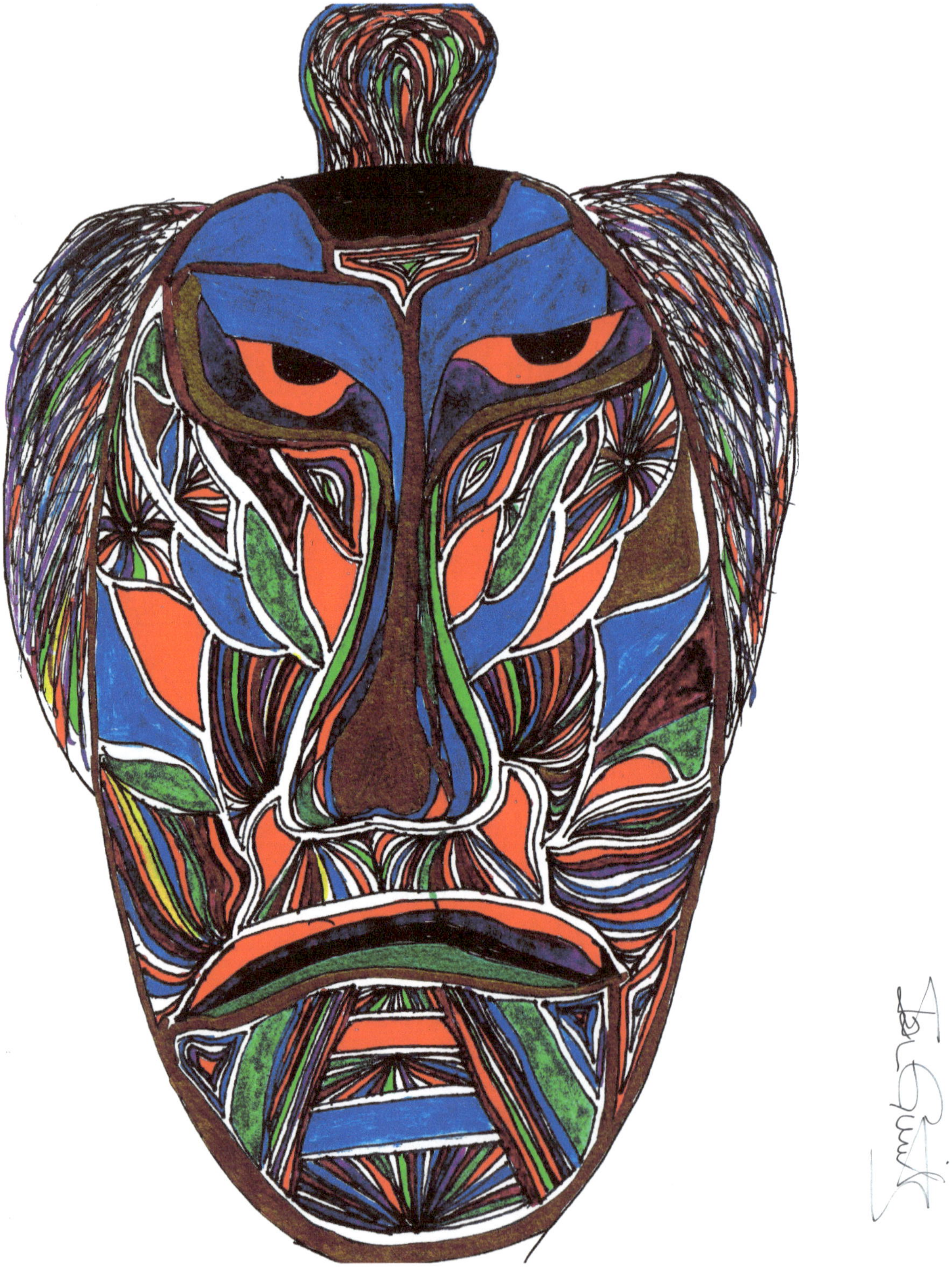

Samurai clown

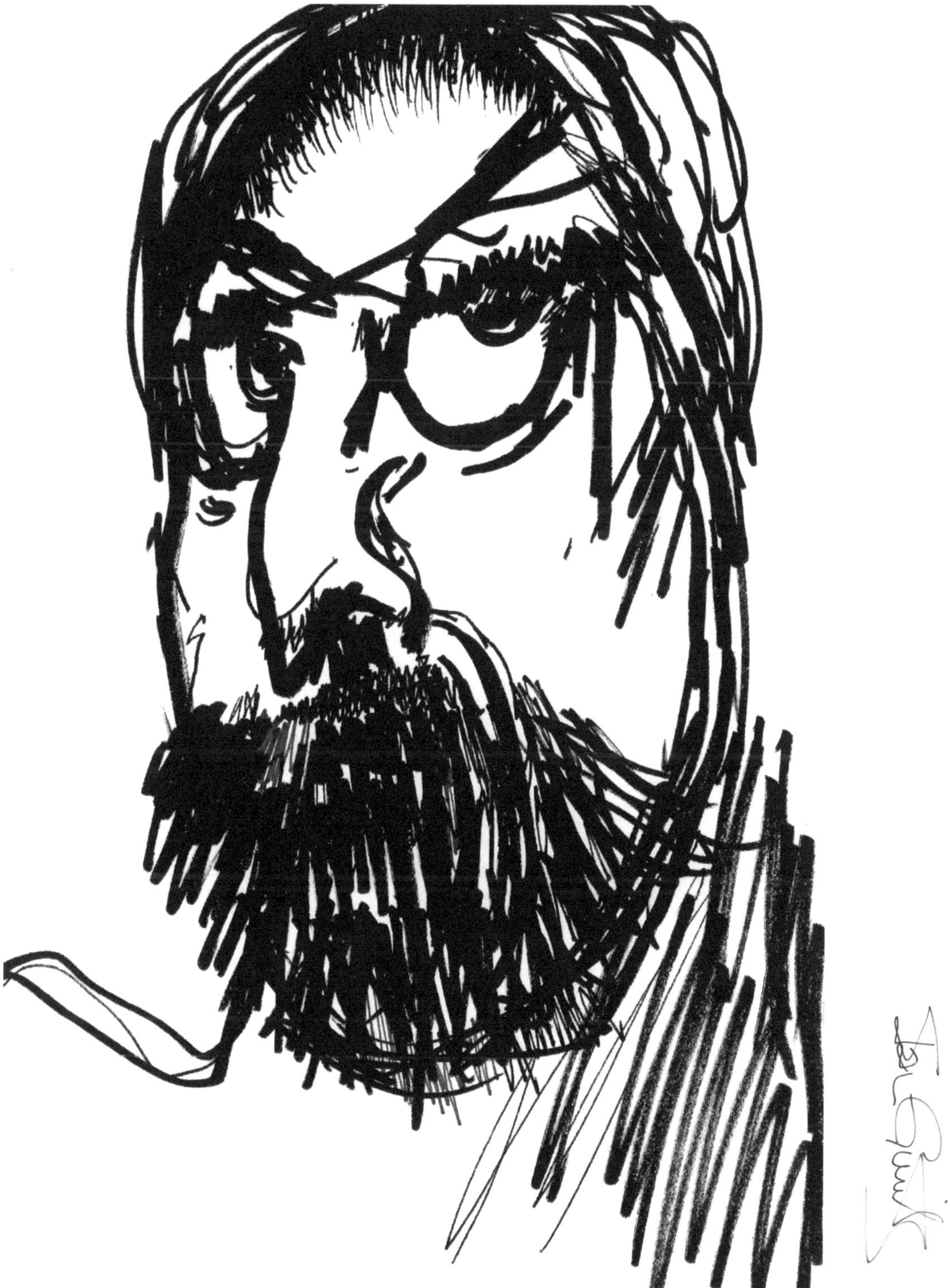

bodhidharma

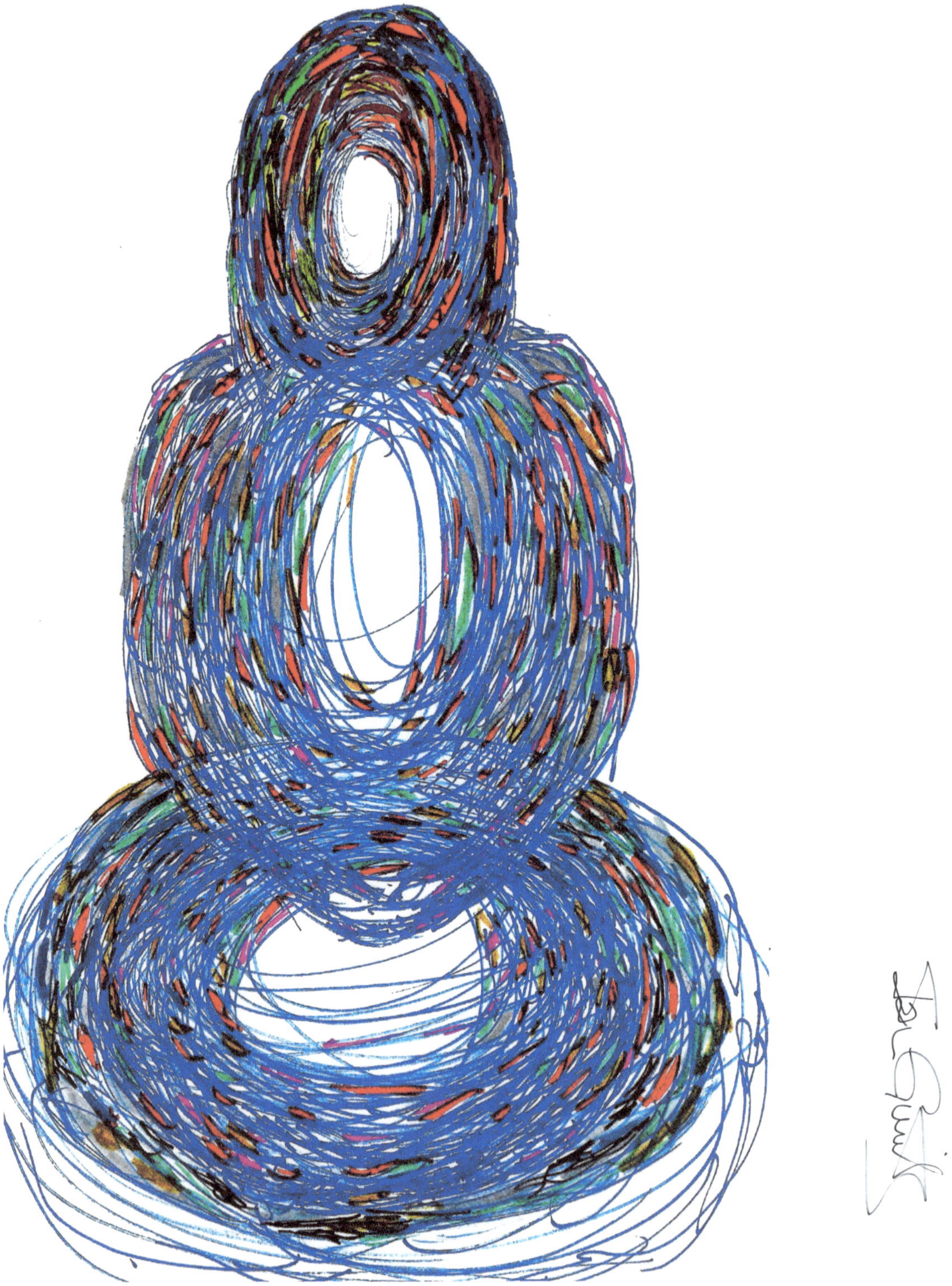

zazen

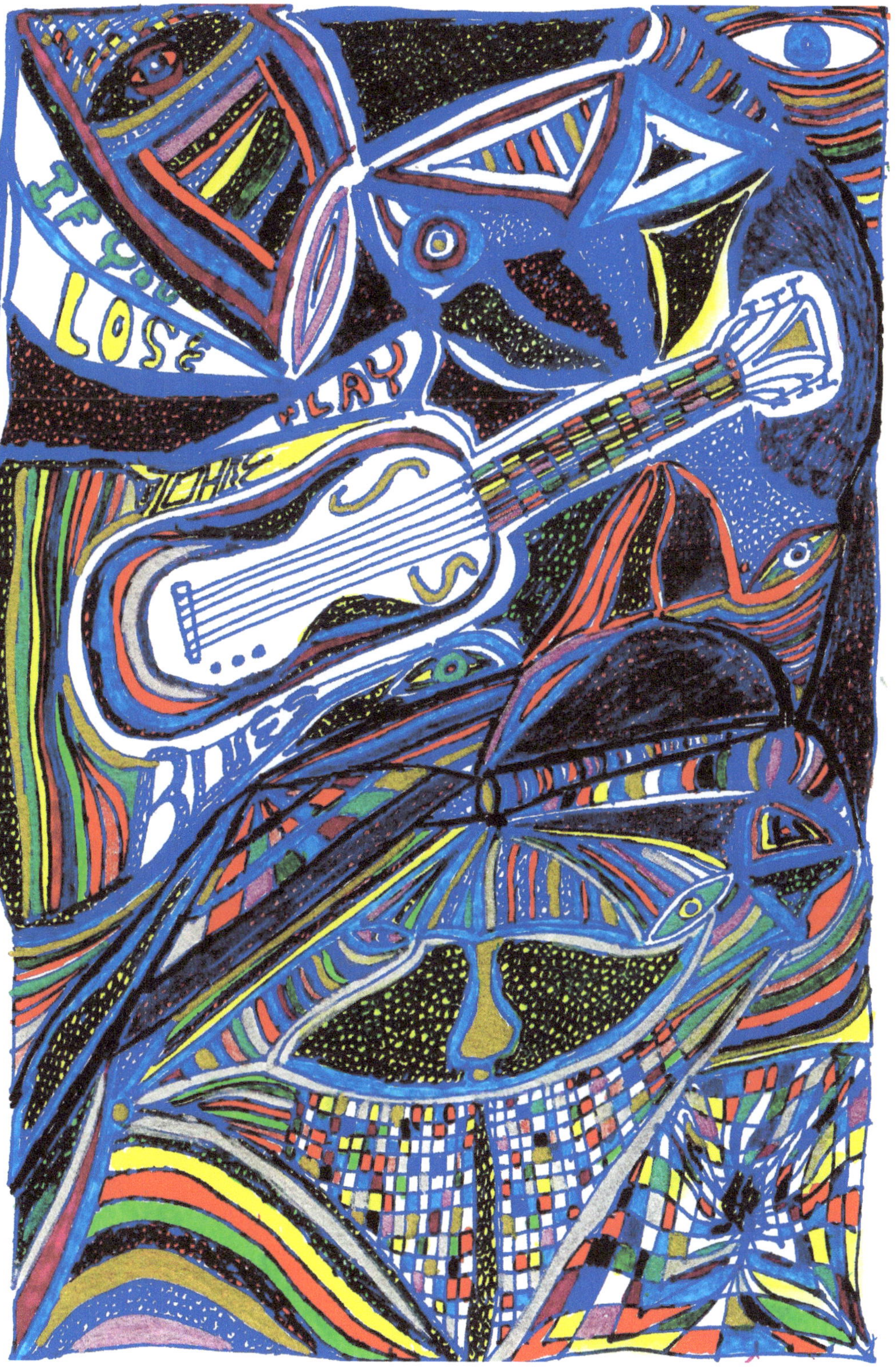


*If you lose, play the blues.*

## talking heads | merchandise

### T-shirts

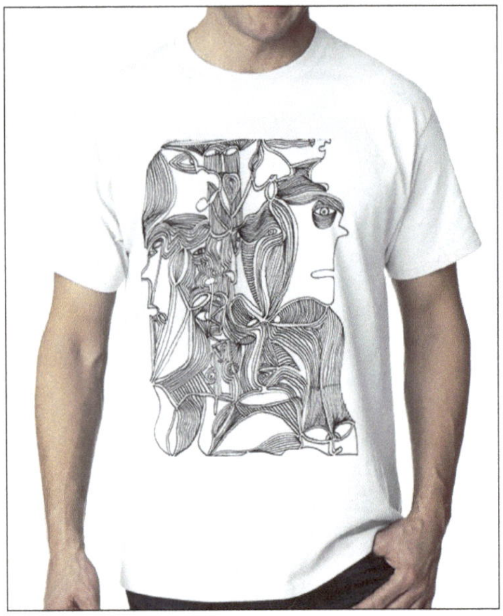

Men's T-shirt M/L/XL
talking heads

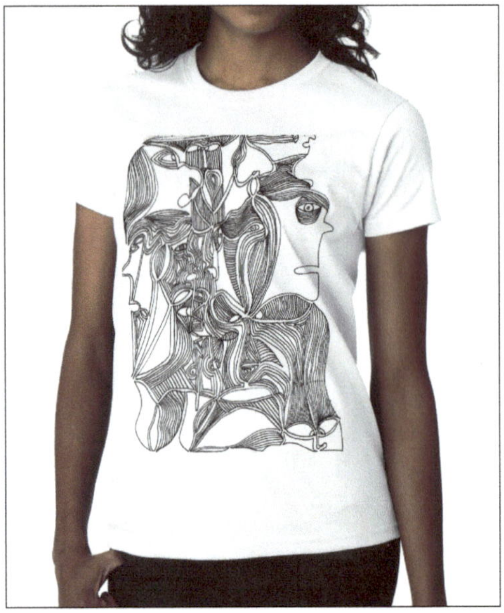

Women's T-shirt M/L/XL
talking heads

Pick any piece from talking heads to put on a mug. See examples below:

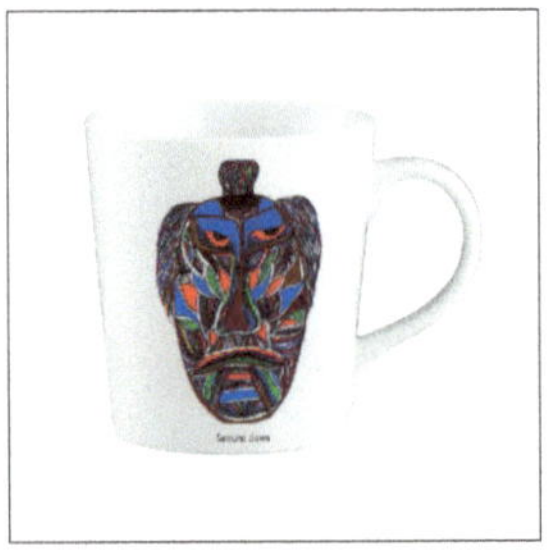

Whitre Ceramic Mug
Samurai clown

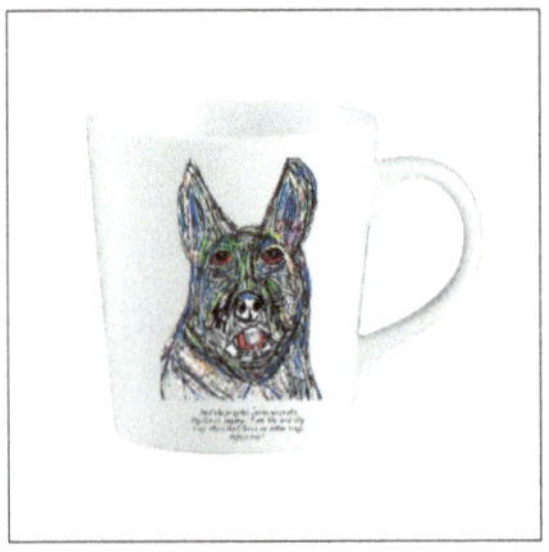

Whitre Ceramic Mug
I am the Lord, thy Dog!

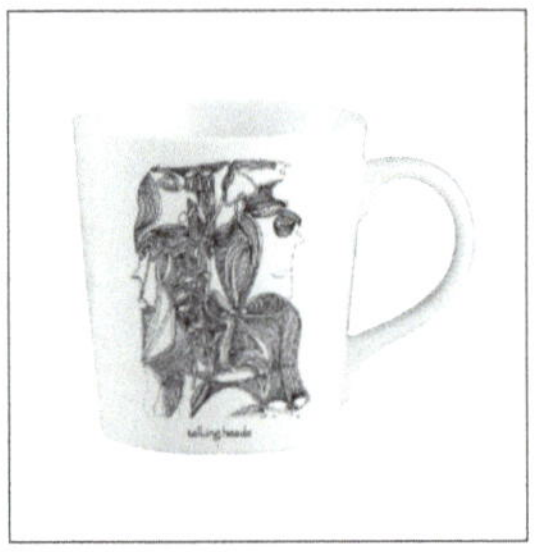

Whitre Ceramic Mug
talking heads

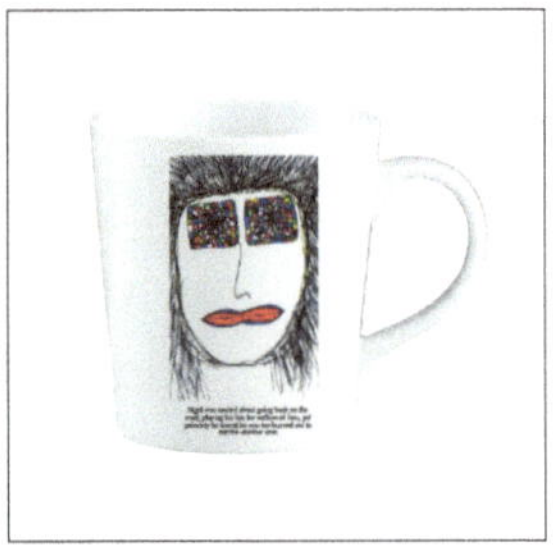

Whitre Ceramic Mug
Nigel on tour

I'm working on making the drawings in this book, as well as many others, available as greeting cards, calendars, posters, mugs, or anything else I can get made.

For requests, or more information, email me talkingheadsbook@gmail.com,
or check out my Facebook page – Talkingheads.
Thank you to Victoria Gapin for her design expertise.

www.ingramcontent.com/pod-product-compliance
Lightning Source LLC
Chambersburg PA
CBHW050800180526
45159CB00004B/1504
*9781539098201*